P9-CMR-885

SEAN
A BIOGRAPHY
CONNERY

SEAN
A BIOGRAPHY
CONNERY
BOB McCABE

THUNDER'S
MOUTH
PRESS

For Lucy, Jessie and Jack – from Finchley with Love

Published in the United States by
Thunder's Mouth Press
841 Broadway, Fourth Floor
New York, NY 10003

First published in Great Britain in 2000 by
PAVILION BOOKS LIMITED
London House, Great Eastern Wharf
Parkgate Road, London SW11 4NQ

Copyright © Essential Books Ltd 2000

All rights reserved. No parts of this publication may be reproduced, stored in a retrieval system,
or transmitted, in any form or by any means, electronic, mechanical, photocopying, recording or
otherwise, without the prior permission of the copyright holder.

Library of Congress Card Number: 00-103999

ISBN 1-56025-290-1

Set in 10/15 Bodoni

Origination by Anglia Graphics, England
Printed and bound in Spain by Bookprint

2 4 6 8 10 9 7 5 3 1

Distributed by Publishers Group West

Contents

'There are seven genuine movie stars in the world and Sean is one of them'

Steven Spielberg

At ease with the world –

Connery heads towards 70 ☆

1. Thomas of Fountainbridge

'It has recently come to light that I have bankability in all places in the world. Some Americans are enormous in the United States, but can't even get arrested elsewhere. It's the bankability which has given me more movies than I've ever had before and the satisfaction is enormous.' Thus spoke Sean Connery in the early 1990s, the beginning of his fifth decade in cinema, one which was to prove just about his most successful and prolific to date.

A few years earlier, when casting him as father figure to 1930s-set hero Indiana Jones – surely a cinematic successor to James Bond if ever there was one – director Steven Spielberg had opined, 'There are seven genuine movie stars in the world today and Sean is one of them.' Now, more than a decade on from both of these comments, as Connery enters his sixth decade as a screen actor and struggles with the burden of having recently been named Sexiest Man of the Last Century, it's hard to imagine one other actor – let alone Spielberg's unnamed half-dozen – sharing the spotlight with Connery.

Former Edinburgh milkman turned super-spy ☆

EXCLUSIVE *Leisure Wear by* VINCE

The New Vince
CAPRI SHIRT
52/6
Plus 1/6 post.

Adapted from the colourful
garb of the Capri Fisherman

*Please state
chest size*

A new and comfortable shirt
with broad shoulders,
inset breast pocket,
ZIPPED side opening
and snug hip fitting
in Black and White
Striped **DENIM**
as illustrated, or
in **BUTCHER
BLUE, FRENCH
GREY, NUTMEG,**
or **WHITE.**

**JEANS
SHORTS**
Italian style with zip front and
two front pockets. In **WHITE
DRILL,** as illus., or in "Faded"
Blue **DENIM.** (State waist size)

25/- Plus 9d. post
NEW 1956 24-page catalogue will be sent on request
Open Mon. Tues. Wed. Fri. 9 to 5.30 p.m.   Thurs. 9 to 7 p.m.   Sat. 9 to 3 p.m.
VINCE MAN'S SHOP (F & F)
5 Newburgh St., Foubert's Place, Regent St., London, W.I.   GERrard 3730
— Come and see our NEW range of leisure wear —

*Sean sells shirts
. . . and shorts* ☆

Age has not withered him; neither has lack of hair, nor his continued insistence on playing everything from a Russian submarine commander to a fourteenth-century monk, from a Prohibition-era Irish-American street cop to the world's most famous Eton-educated spy, all complete with a thick Edinburgh accent.

Instead, Sean Connery has grown in stature, both as an actor and as that most ephemeral of beings, a movie star.

But not for him the resting on his considerable laurels and an elder statesman status based solely on the fact that, as he turns seventy, he's still among us. And still active.

Connery has instead crafted a career based on a subtle redefining of image, that has allowed him to move from sex symbol to character actor, from reborn hero to respected father figure, from adventurer in his youth, to adventurer in his middle age and beyond.

No other movie star in the history of cinema has so successfully crossed gender lines – women want him, men want to be him – for so protracted a period of time. From the age of thirty-two, when he first assumed the mantle of 007, to his seventieth year, Connery's magnetism has never wavered, as his acting prowess has continued to grow.

In short, Sean Connery is a star like no other, before or since.

This unique individuality, however, was by no means reflected in the birthplace and early life of one Thomas Connery, delivered unto parents Joe and Effie on the morning of 25 August 1930.

The name Fountainbridge conjures all manner of mystical thoughts, but in reality the street which gave its name to the surrounding area in Connery's native Edinburgh was a dark, functional place. Tenement buildings, including the Connerys' at 176 Fountainbridge, housed dozens of families of all sizes in cramped two-roomed conditions. The grandeur of Edinburgh Castle may have been viewable in the distance, but closer to home was the permanent smell of hops fermenting at the McEwan's brewery at one end of the street, and the seemingly endless black smoke from the North British Rubber Company factory bordering the other end. A hundred yards away lay the Grand

Union Canal, once a hive of commercial activity, now little more than a place for the local kids to fish in. The locals referred to their area as Auld Reekie – Old Smoke.

In later years, of course, the impoverished beginnings of the man who would be movie star attained an inevitable rose-tinted quality, but in reality Fountainbridge was a financially deprived stretch of slum housing. It remained bound together only by its strong sense of community, borne in part out of both a shared poverty and shared bathroom facilities.

Joe Connery's father was an Irish tinker from County Wexford, but Joe considered himself a Scotsman first and foremost. During the Depression, he took whatever work he could find, be it occasional labour at the local rubber company, or long-distance lorry driving. He considered moving south, looking for better employment, but Effie liked the community feel of Fountainbridge, the inter-mingling lives of those on 'the stair' as the locals called it.

Their first son, Thomas – later Sean – arrived that August and spent his early months sharing his parents' room, sleeping in the bottom drawer of their wardrobe. He later graduated to a fold-out bed put up every night in the kitchen, a room he continued to occupy on frequent visits back home long after he had moved away. He was keen on football, less so on academic work and was joined – first in the bottom drawer, later on another put-up bed in the kitchen – by a brother, Neil, in 1938.

The arrival of a sibling awakened in young Thomas two notions that were firmly to remain with him throughout his life – a sense of responsibility, and an abiding interest and understanding of all matters fiscal. Joe Connery brought home £6 a week – not a bad sum for those on the stair. Effie cleaned for a further fifteen shillings, but now there was an extra mouth to feed, so young Tommy decided it was time he pulled his weight.

'My family was poor,' he later rationalized. 'My father was a long-distance lorry driver, and my mother a char. I started working from the time I was nine, delivering milk seven days a week, as well as going to school.'

He landed a job at the local St Cuthbert's Dairy Stables, just around the corner from his home, in Grove Street. The job entailed lugging crates of milk up numerous flights of stairs every morning, and his wages were always – willingly – handed over to his mother. In addition Tommy earned pocket money from a local paper round and part-time work for the local butcher.

'I never thought of myself as underprivileged,' he later remarked. 'I started to work when I was nine. It was probably good training, because when I finally left home, I was already formed in terms of taking care of myself. My folks were not too concerned about how I was going to do it.'

Joe Connery went to work for Rolls-Royce in Glasgow, which meant better money, but also being away from his family during the week, only making the forty-mile journey back at weekends. Tommy, about to start secondary school, naturally thought of himself as the man of the house on weekdays.

There were two schools available to the local children of Fountainbridge in the early 1940s – World War II permitting. If a child showed particular aptitude at primary school, they went on to Boroughmuir; if they didn't, the choice was Darroch. Tommy Connery went to Darroch. This was fine by Connery, who showed much more interest in both football and paid work.

Some weekends offered escape from the grim Edinburgh environs. Trips to maternal grand-parents Neil and Helen McLean out in the country-side of Dunfermline became a highlight for both the Connery boys, what with fresh spring water, eggs from the local farm and plenty of wide open spaces in which to kick a ball about.

Other moments of escape from tenement living came via the local cinema, the Blue Hills. Young Tommy especially favoured the Flash Gordon serials with Buster Crabbe and American westerns. Working part-time at the dairy was earning Tommy

fifteen shillings a week. With a war on, he knew it wasn't enough. 'In 1941 and 1942 the educational system in Scotland became very erratic,' he has said. 'Schools were closed. We were taught in people's houses – when we could be taught. You see, children were being evacuated to Australia, or wherever else there was safety from the bombing. My birthday, which is 25 August, was near the end of school summer holidays. So, in 1943, the year I was thirteen, when school closed for the summer vacation, I never went back. Instead, I got a job driving a horse, delivering milk, because all the men were in the services.'

Thomas Connery became a milkman full-time. The rise in his fortunes was instant and profound – his salary leapt to £2 14s, once again faithfully handed over to his mother, Connery keeping the additional five shillings he earned from his paper round for himself.

Full-time employment came with the added attraction of his own horse, Tich, which Connery lovingly groomed and cared for.

Joe Connery was injured at work in Glasgow and was unable to find work for many months afterwards, leaving the family even more dependent on Tommy's earnings. By the age of fourteen, the youngster was doing three jobs a day, dawn to dusk.

Still, there was always the occasional game of football. A love of the game, and an impressive

SEAN CONNERY

Models

MATELOT VESTS

Imported from France in
Traditional Blue and White Stripes

29/6 *each. Plus 9d. post*

BLUE JEANS

in "Washed Out" Denim
Zip front, 2 hip and 2 front pockets

42/- *per pair. Plus 1/6 post*

Open Mon. Tues. Wed. Fri., 9 to 5.30 p.m.
Thurs, 9 to 7 p.m.
and Sats. 9 to 3 p.m.

VINCE man's shop (F & F)
5 NEWBURGH STREET · FOUBERTS PLACE · REGENT STREET · LONDON W1 · GERRARD 3730

Connery goes commercial, early 1950s ☆

physique, borne in part out of years of carrying milk crates and hard labour, gave young Connery a reputation as a strong, athletic youngster. His height rapidly approaching six foot two merely added to his impressive physical countenance, and he was soon known by the nickname of 'Big Tam'. At weekends, he played soccer for Grove Vale Juvenile, later moving on to Oxgangs Rovers. 'I started as a halfback, then I ended up as a forward, because although I was big, I was quick.' He later turned professional and played for the Scottish team, Bonnyrig Rose Athletic, where he was scouted by East Fife who offered him a £25 signing fee, which Connery rejected.

Big Tam was surprised one day to find that his mother, despite their impoverished means, had been putting money aside in a post office account

for her son. Tommy added to these savings and by the age of sixteen, the account had grown to a substantial £75. Finally, after years of hard work, here was something that Tommy could indulge himself with. His first desire was to buy a motorbike, but this decision led to an argument with his father. The young Connery passed on the bike, but returned home one day with £56-worth of piano – a status symbol on the stair undoubtedly, but not one that any member of his immediate family could play.

There was the daily slog, some money in his pocket, parading down the local palais and, due to his striking good looks, a growing reputation among the young women of Edinburgh. But it wasn't enough. Tommy Connery wanted to see the world, but, seemingly trapped in post-war

Scotland, he had no idea how to do it. So, having joined the sea cadets at school, Connery decided to go one step further and joined the navy.

'Today, it would be considered foolish by many, I know,' he once recalled. 'Coming from my own particular background though, I felt I was getting rather a good deal by going into the navy. Employment, clothes, food, all that. I couldn't wait to go to sea.'

Connery travelled across the Firth to the naval shore-base of HMS *Lochinvar* and signed up for seven years active service and five in the reserves. He thought he was off to see the world; instead he was off to see Portsmouth. And more than his share of navy doctors. Having been trained as an armourer, Connery was posted to HMS *Formidable* at Portsmouth. He decided that he would mark the occasion in the traditional manner; by acquiring two tattoos on his arms – one reading 'Mum & Dad', the other 'Scotland Forever'.

His time onboard ship, though, was not a pleasant one. After several years as a fiercely independent young man, he found the regulation of navy life intensely restrictive, to the point where he developed increasingly problematic stomach pains. Three years after signing on, Able Seaman Connery was placed in the naval hospital for two months, suffering from duodenal ulcers brought on by stress. He was, upon recovery, invalided out on a pension

of six shillings and eight pence a week, less than half what he'd earned from his first job as a part-time milkman.

Once again Tommy Connery, now nineteen, found himself back sleeping in his parents' kitchen at Fountainbridge, wondering what to do with his life. This was a restless period for Connery. His first job back in Civvy Street was as a coalman; he quit after three weeks, deciding this was not the life for him. A steel-working job lasted two months, a stint as a road worker was equally short-lived.

The obvious answer was to train or apprentice at one of the, admittedly limited, local trades available, via a scheme funded by the local British Legion. Big Tam opted for french polishing and landed a job with a local cabinet maker's firm, where he inadvertently got his first experience in the theatre – a fellow worker alerted him to the fact that the nearby King's Theatre hired in strong young lads for backstage work, especially during the prestigious Edinburgh Festival. Connery signed on for a few extra pounds a week and a glimpse of another life.

The day job, meanwhile, left him polishing coffins for a local undertaker.

In weighing up what he had available to him, Connery became aware of one major asset. And how to exploit it. From years of manual labour,

Number 24, posing pouch and all, in the Mr Universe contest, 1953 ☆

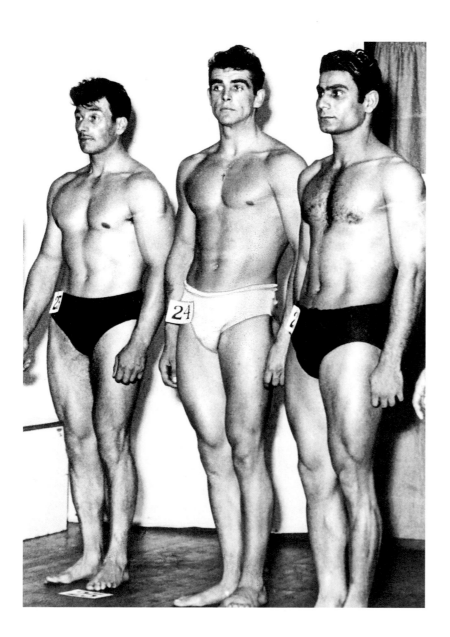

Connery had developed a strong and impressive physique. He wasn't called Big Tam for nothing!

So he doffed workclothes and donned a G-string to become a model at Edinburgh University life-drawing classes.

The awareness that his physical appearance could earn him money coincided with Connery reading about a man named Jimmy Laurie, a Scottish physical fitness trainer and body-builder. Connery decided to track Laurie down and, under his guidance, became a member of the Dunedin Amateur Weight Lifting Club. Here he spent many hours, toning his muscles and stature.

He continued to model for the university classes, and in addition travelled south to Manchester, on his newly purchased motorbike, to do photographic work for Vince Studios, appearing in a series of magazine fashion adverts in the early 1950s.

He also worked briefly as a bouncer at the local dance hall before landing his first job on stage. Replying to an advert in the local paper requiring men over six feet tall, Connery was hired as an extra in a touring production of *The Glorious Years*, starring Anna Neagle. 'I stood around on that stage for five weeks dressed as a guards officer,' he once recalled. 'I only got the job because they wanted someone tall.' He did not fall in love with the theatre, he was merely grateful for what seemed to be easy money.

During the summer, Connery worked as a lifeguard at the Portobello pool, a large open-air salt-water pool, where the six-foot-two muscular Connery proved a definite hit with the ladies. Not that sex seemed to be an issue for the sex symbol to be, who later claimed to have been introduced to the subject from a very early age. 'I was eight years old and it was a lurid introduction to sex, but pretty basic. Although I can't remember a particular moment when I lost my virginity, it was a gradual acceptance that I no longer had it. I was never successful with ladies early on despite my knowledge. I was very shy.'

With lifeguard work restricted to the summer time, Connery took yet another day job – cleaning presses at the *Edinburgh Evening News*.

Back at the Dunedin Amateur Weight Lifting Club, however, Jimmy Laurie was formulating a plan that was to prove one of the major turning points of Tommy Connery's life. The Mr Universe contest was being held in London that year and both he and his friend Connery were going to enter and represent Scotland.

Connery, already aware of how to hold and present his body courtesy of his experience as a life model, studiously practised the required poses, before making his first trip to London.

The contest was held at the Scala Theatre and Connery was placed third in his class, winning a bronze medal. 'I looked like Ronnie Corbett next to the fella that won,' he joked. 'The Americans were mountainous. Their arms were like my legs.'

However, it was only the size of the American winners that impressed the Scot. 'It was quite a disillusionment for me to meet them,' he recalled in 1974, 'because at the club I went to in Edinburgh, we were all very health and strength-conscious. But the Americans and the London fellas seemed to be solely intent on acquiring inches and bulk. I was absolutely shattered to discover that somebody wouldn't run for a bus because he might lose some of his bulk. But just to be a bulky physique would be boring to me – not to run, not to play football, not to swim: a cul-de-sac.'

Connery may have been disappointed with his close-up view of the world of professional body-building, but had he never entered the contest in the first place, his life would have taken a very different course. 'Several of the entrants in the Mr Universe contest were in the *South Pacific* company, which was then in the last three months of its run at Drury Lane. After that they were going on tour, and some cast replacements were coming up. So they told me about this and I went to audition. I practised for two days, sang a sailor's shanty and got a part.'

Connery walked on the stage and firmly answered 'Yes' when asked if he was an actor and

SOUTH PACIFIC

CAST

(In order of their appearance)

NGANA	{ JUDITH MANNING or { SHIRLEY EMERY
JEROME	{ MICHAEL BARNETT or { RONALD SINGER
HENRY	...CHICK ALEXANDER
ENSIGN NELLIE FORBUSH	JULIE WILSON
EMILE DE BECQUE	WILBUR EVANS
BLOODY MARY	MURIEL SMITH
BLOODY MARY'S ASSISTANT	HELEN LANDIS
STEWPOT	JOHN ORCHARD
LUTHER BILLIS	... COLIN CROFT
PROFESSOR	PAUL DOBSON
LT. JOSEPH CABLE, U.S.M.C. ...	DAVID WILLIAMS
CAPT. GEORGE BRACKETT, U.S.N.	JOHN McLAREN
CMDR. WILLIAM HARBISON, U.S.N.	JOHN HARVEY
YEOMAN HERBERT QUALE	FRANKLIN FOX
ABNER	ABE ELLIS
SGT. KENNETH JOHNSON	IVOR EMANUEL
SEABEE RICHARD WEST	HENRY GOODIER
SEABEE MORTON WISE	PETER WHITAKER
SEAMAN TOM O'BRIEN...	ADRIAN DESMOND
RADIO OPERATOR BOB McCAFFREY	FRANKLIN FOX
MARINE CPL. HAMILTON STEEVES ...	ROLAND GREEN
STAFF SGT. THOMAS HASSINGER ...	GORDON DOBSON
PT. SVEN LARSEN	ANDREW COLE
PT. VICTOR JEROME	DESMOND D'ARCY
SGT. WATERS	HAYES NICHOLAS
LT. GENEVIEVE MARSHALL ...	PATRICIA HARTLEY
ENSIGN DINAH MURPHY	GLORIA GEORGE
ENSIGN JANET MacGREGOR ...	BRENDA BARKER
ENSIGN CORA MacRAE	MAUREEN GRANT
ENSIGN SUE YAEGER	CAROLE LESLIE
ENSIGN LISA MINELLI	MELA WHITE
ENSIGN CONNIE WALEWSKA ...	JANE BOLTON
ENSIGN PAMELA WHITMORE ...	JASMINE LINDSAY
ENSIGN BESSIE NOONAN	JANE HILL
ENSIGN BETTY PITT	ROSALIE WHITHAM
LIAT	CHIN YU
MARCEL (Henry's Assistant)	LLOYD RECKORD
LT. BUZZ ADAMS	NEVIL WHITING
Islanders, Sailors, Marines, Officers : STANLEY HOWLETT, SEAN CONNERY	

Bottom of the bill, Sean Connery's professional stage debut, South Pacific, Drury Lane, 1953 ☆

whether he could sing and dance or not. He then dropped the pages he was supposed to be reading from. 'Hurry up. We haven't got all day,' came a distant voice, from the darkened stalls.

'Neither have I,' replied the annoyed Scot, before storming off.

Intrigued, the producer called him back and had him read. Noting the impressive span of his shoulders, Connery landed a part in the chorus. Still standing on the stage, and ever mindful of the money involved, the Scot then asked what his wage would be.

'It doesn't concern me,' answered the producer, used to having an underling deal with such matters.

'Well, it concerns me,' Connery replied, and soon learned that he would be picking up a not inconsiderable £12 a week.

He returned to Edinburgh with a bronze medal and the news that he was to spend the next year of his life touring the country as part of the cast of *South Pacific*.

Although Connery was impressed – as were those back in Fountainbridge – by the glamour of his new job, he still didn't view it as a career. The notion of becoming an actor seemed far less important to him at first than the opportunity finally to see at least a small part of the world. 'All it meant to me was a chance to tour Britain, get twice as much money as I'd ever earned before and only work for a couple of hours a night.'

In later years, of course, Connery looked back on winning that job in the chorus as the most significant event of his career. 'It altered the course of my life', he stated simply in 1995.

For most of his life, and despite the close support of his family, Tommy Connery had never fitted in. Yes, he played football with the other kids and yes, he was part of the extended family of those on the stair, but always he looked for something more than that. He worked out of necessity, but, bar his horse Tich, the work was always purely functional, rarely enjoyable. In essence, he began his adult life with an attempt to get away from his youth, by joining the navy, instinctively knowing there was something out there, something more than a wage packet at the end of the week and Saturday night in the pub. 'My father's family was part tinker, so perhaps there's something about that which prompts me to feel that I should always be going somewhere, moving somewhere, rather than staying where I am.'

In the theatre, Connery finally found what he was looking for, although during his first weeks on tour Connery did not mix easily with his fellow cast members. Then he realized why. 'It all came out later,' he once recalled. 'The queer looks I was getting were because of my Scots accent. They thought I was Polish. They couldn't understand a word I said.'

Nonetheless, Connery was up there on stage, dressed as an American marine, singing along with 'There Is Nothin' Like a Dame' every night.

Two significant events happened during the run of *South Pacific*. First, Thomas changed his name to Sean, long believed to be in reference to his local nickname of Shane, named after the Alan Ladd western. The second event was Sean Connery meeting Robert Henderson. An older, American actor in the show, more than anyone else up to that time, Henderson saw the potential in Connery.

'I said, "Acting? What do I know about acting?" I told him, "I can sing 'Nothin' Like a Dame', I can

do handsprings on the stage." Frankly, I was happy just to get my £12 a week and drive around.'

Life on the road was fun and fine, but, with Henderson's encouragement, Connery began to realize that becoming an actor, a real actor, was not only a possibility but a genuine desire for him. 'It wasn't until I decided to become an actor that I really began to do something with my life.'

Henderson began his unofficial mentoring of the Scot by providing him with a list of books that any actor worth his salt should have read. They included such titles as Tolstoy's *War and Peace*, James Joyce's *Finnegans Wake* and *Ulysses*, Thomas Wolfe's *Look Homeward Angel* and Proust's *Remembrance of Things Past*.

Connery made straight for the local libraries in whichever town the company found themselves in and began to devour Henderson's list, which was rapidly growing, throwing in the plays of Shakespeare, Ibsen, Shaw and Wilde for good measure. 'I was like a mole digging my way through the world's literature,' Connery affectionately recalled. 'To be an actor, you need to able to look like a miner, and to have read Proust.'

Whatever Connery was going to do, he was going to do well, so he spent his afternoons visiting the local repertory theatre of whatever town they were playing, watching the shows and observing and learning from the actors he saw. 'I was very

Making his big screen debut in 1956's No Road Back ☆

impressed initially with their brilliance. As they went on, I came to realize that this was absolute nonsense. I had imbued them with talents they didn't have.'

One potential distraction from his zealous new life came when he was spotted playing football with some of the other cast members by a scout from Manchester United, then, under the legendary eye of Matt Busby, the greatest team in football. 'The show was nine weeks in Manchester,' said Connery, 'and at that time I was in a football team made up from the cast. And I was asked if I would consider playing for Manchester United. I was only twenty-three then. I decided against it, really, after talking it over with Robert Henderson. That was when I knew I wanted to become an actor.'

Weighing up the options, Connery reasoned that a professional footballer's career wouldn't extend much past his thirtieth birthday, while, as Henderson pointed out to his protégé, an actor can go on for ever. Connery went with the long-term plan, investing in a large Grundig reel-to-reel tape recorder, into which he read Shakespeare, working on his diction, softening his accent. He never sought to lose his accent, however, something that would come to define him on film and probably make him one of the most imitated actors in cinema history. Robert Henderson once recalled, 'He started off with a Scots accent that was so thick it was like a foreign accent. He cured himself of that, but think of the study it took! He worked and sweated blood.'

Connery's perseverance was rewarded later in the show's run, when he started to understudy two small, speaking roles in the play. By the time the show hit Edinburgh, the newly christened Sean Connery was billed in the programme as Lt Buzz Adams. The home-town audience were impressed.

Having now settled on his chosen profession,

Stanley Baker, James Bond, Danger Man and the star of Bless This House – *together at last!* – Hell Drivers *(1956)* ☆

Sean Connery found himself unemployed at the end of *South Pacific*'s year-long run. He moved to London, lived off what little savings he had amassed, sold his motorbike, opting for a rusty old bicycle, and went to audition after audition. But, as Connery later said, this was to prove to be his 'too' period – 'I was too tall or too big, too Scottish, or too Irish, too young or too old.'

To supplement his dole, Connery would take all manner of odd jobs, including babysitting for Peter Noble, the late news columnist for the film industry trade paper *Screen International*. As Noble once recalled, 'He was a bit hard-up at the time and for ten bob he agreed to look after the baby. If he had to change a nappy he got another ten bob, and there

were times when we'd come back and he'd say, "I've had to change a nappy twice tonight," so he got thirty bob.'

Connery was at this time living near the Nobles, in Brondesbury Villas, the Kilburn end of Abbey Road, renting a room from journalist Llew Gardner and his wife Merry Archard. The room had come to Connery's attention via one of Ms Archard's colleagues, a twenty-one-year-old photographer named Julie Hamilton. Hamilton was the daughter of writer Jill Craigie, wife of Labour politician Michael Foot, and she and the struggling actor were soon an item.

Work was practically non-existent for Connery during this period, with one failed audition after another, although at least now he was failing auditions for movies – he was deemed too tall for Twentieth Century–Fox's *Boy on a Dolphin*, and too dark for Rank's *High Tide at Noon*.

His old mentor Robert Henderson offered a brief respite from the dole office – in the shape of a non-speaking walk-on part in a production of Agatha Christie's *Witness for the Prosecution* that he was directing at the Kew Theatre. The Old Vic were less amenable, rejecting the Scot and recommending he take elocution lessons.

Small roles were snared in further productions at the Kew – Jean Anouilh's *Point of Departure* and Dolph Norman's *A Witch in Time*. He was spotted during these productions by a director from the Oxford Playhouse, who offered him the role of Pentheus in a production of Euripides' *The Bacchae*. He returned to Oxford later that season to appear in Eugene O'Neill's *Anna Christie*.

More theatre work followed upon his return to London, with a small role in *The Good Sailor* at the Lyric Theatre in Hammersmith.

It was also during this lean period that Connery made his motion-picture debut, albeit as an extra in 1954's *Lilacs in the Spring*, starring Anna Neagle.

Television, however, was proving kinder to Connery, even if his statuesque physique meant he was mostly being offered brawn rather than brain parts. He played a villain in an episode of the popular police drama *Dixon of Dock Green*, a smuggler in the Lorne Green-starring *Sailor of Fortune* and, more incongruously, an aggressive Italian porter in *The Jack Benny Show* for the BBC.

Connery made his official motion-picture debut – yes, he had lines to speak and everything – in the instantly forgettable 1956 B-movie crime drama *No Road Back*. Once again, the actor was cast principally on his looks and build, playing Alfie Bass's muscle. Bass introduced himself to the movie debutant by instantly setting him up – he strongly suggested that Connery should have words with the director about his character's weak dialogue and permanent stutter. Connery took the bait and stormed off to confront Montgomery Tully, only to discover that the director was also the co-writer of the film and that he suffered from a noticeable speech impediment.

No Road Back was duly completed and released, promptly flopped and is best forgotten. The same could probably be said of Connery's second movie, were it not for the fact that it makes for a great movie-quiz trivia question: Which film featured James Bond, Danger Man, Ilya Kuryakin, the first Dr Who AND Sid James? Answer: 1956's tale of fast-driving truckers, *Hell Drivers*, which cast the likes of Connery, Patrick McGoohan, David McCallum, William Hartnell and the 'Carry On' alumnus alongside the film's star, Stanley Baker.

In no position to choose his roles, Connery next appeared – all muscle again – in the somewhat less than starry role of 'Second Welder' in the child-trapped-in-a-vault melodrama *Time Lock*, notable now only for the fact that it was made by the team of Gerald Thomas and Peter Rogers, who, one year later, would for ever change the face of British screen comedy – for better and worse – with the launch of the 'Carry On' films.

This was followed by the adventure flick, *Action of the Tiger*. During production, Connery had high hopes that this movie could really take off and approached director Terence Young, naively enquiring, 'Sir, am I going to be a success in this?' The director's answer was a plain 'no', but he promised to make it up to him – Young later directed the first James Bond adventure, *Dr No*.

It was on the small screen, however, that the developing actor would find his first real break. Once again, it was a role that his physicality helped him land, but here, for the first time, was a chance for Connery to show the increasing depth of his talent. *Requiem for a Heavyweight*, the tragic tale of a washed-up boxer named Mountain McClintock, written by *Twilight Zone* creator Rod Serling, remains one of the classics of early American television. Originally aired live in 1953, it starred Jack Palance in fine form as the crumbling pugilist.

The BBC now planned to broadcast their own live version of the play, and were flying Palance in to reprise his acclaimed role. Ten days before the 31 March 1957 air date, Palance backed out of the project due to other work commitments. Producer Alvin Rakoff was desperate for a replacement, when his wife Jacqueline Hill – cast as the female lead in the piece – suggested Connery. Rakoff had previously cast Connery in three small parts in his production *The Condemned*, but was sceptical about giving him such a prominent role.

It was a hell of a gamble – and just what Connery had been looking for. After a short reading, Rakoff decided and called Connery to tell him the news. 'What I especially remember about the phone call was that Connery was tremendously grateful,' the producer once recalled. 'I think that he instinctively knew that this was a major role, the first of his life, and he could make something of it. So did I.'

A week of intense rehearsal followed – a young actor named Michael Caine was cast in a bit part in the final scene – and on Sunday night it aired, and was deemed a huge success, with Connery finally attracting the attention of both the audience and the critics. Not only that, his dad was impressed as well – 'By heavens, that was smashing,' declared Joe Connery, crowded round a tiny television set back in Fountainbridge that Sunday evening.

By Monday morning, things had started moving.

Even in his early films, Sean Connery had a way with the ladies – here with Martine Carol in Action of the Tiger *(1957)* ☆

Connery and future wife
Diane Cilento attend the
premiere of Sleeping
Beauty, *1959* ☆

'I must have received two hundred offers the next day,' Connery later recalled. 'I think I had every casting director in London knocking on my door. It was quite a part considering I had to talk through a gum shield for ninety minutes. And all for £35.'

Among the potential deals were contract offers from Rank films and Twentieth Century-Fox. Rather than leap at either opportunity – and this was an opportunity that Connery had been waiting several years to get – the actor decided to take a week-long holiday, driving to Scotland with Julie Hamilton, to weigh up his deals and decide how best to manage his career.

Connery's landlord, Llew Gardner, later recalled: 'Here was a young man being offered contracts that in the eyes of most struggling actors would look like three lemons in the window of a one-armed bandit, and treating them as though any well-muscled, weightlifting ex-milkman from Scotland could expect no less.'

'I went round to every company – canny Scot that I am – to see which one would offer the best deal,' Connery later said. 'I used to live in a basement and eat spaghetti and nothing else for weeks because that was all I could afford. And if necessary I'll go back to that.'

Rank may have been the biggest player in the British film industry, but Twentieth Century–Fox were American and consequently global. If Connery was intent on making himself a star – and that was clearly his intention – then Fox seemed the logical offer to take. He signed up for seven years, receiving a weekly retainer and, almost from the off, rejecting nearly everything they sent his way. Any guilt he may have felt over taking their money while essentially doing little or nothing for them in return, did not stop Connery moving into a mews flat in St John's Wood.

The relationship with Julie Hamilton ended later that year, shortly after Connery's next major TV role. In the ITV production of O'Neill's *Anna Christie*, broadcast that August, Connery played the role of Mat Burke, the same part he had played at the Oxford Playhouse the year before. This time, his leading lady was a young Australian-born actress, Diane Cilento, destined to become the first Mrs Sean Connery.

Throughout his early career, Connery was slowly but surely reinventing himself. Having developed his strength and physique, in part as a result of years of muscle-building manual labour, Connery knew innately how to exploit it. Indeed, it was what got him a foothold in the acting world in the first place. But once inside, he quickly realized it was not enough. So he set about a vigorous course of intellectual reinvention, schooling himself in the reference points this new world needed, and which he sorely lacked. Steadfastly ignoring the option of drama school and formal training, he trained himself, working for hours on understanding how his voice and accent affected and influenced his performance, hearing his speech as others would hear it via his Grundig tape recorder. In addition, he relentlessly studied other actors, watching stage performances whenever he could, noticing details, absorbing them. At the cinema, he studied Brando, assessed the American's 'method' approach, took what he wanted from it, and threw away the histrionics. He was assiduously building the being that was Sean Connery – the actor. For all his raw power and considerable sensuality and charisma, there was under it all, an actor awash with technique. Cilento provided the final piece.

Commenting on what she considered to be his stodgy movement during *Anna Christie*, Cilento suggested a man who could help. Yat Malmgren was a Swedish yoga specialist, originally a dancer in the Kurt Jooss Ballet Company. Cilento herself was a client, and Connery studied with Malmgren for the next three years. 'He taught the study of action – attitudes and drives,' Connery recalled in a mid-seventies interview. 'It was based on the concepts of time and motion evolved by the Hungarian dancer Rudolf von Laban. I used to go three to four times a week doing the physical, and three times a week doing the theory. We learned a

cohesive terminology that applied to the whole group, so that there was no problem of communication as there so often is with expressions that mean one thing to one person and another to somebody else. It was a remarkable period for me. It proved that with the proper exercises you can reshape your physical structure. Nothing like the weightlifting exercises I'd done, but attacking yourself from within, from the head through to the base of the spine – to awaken yourself physically, completely, so that you become a much better tuned instrument.'

'When I taught him,' Malmgren (who later instructed another man who would be Bond, Pierce Brosnan) recalled to *Premiere* magazine, 'I told him, "If Clark Gable can do it, you can too." The acting was always more or less the same – he has done many films, but not that many character variations – but what Sean has is that he believes in the situation and everyone seems to love him for that.'

'The first question a spectator asks at a play or a film is "what are they up to?" ' Connery explained. 'I believe you understand eighty per cent of the play just from the movement. Which is a really good test of acting. If you can show what people are doing, then the dialogue and the sound effects become like a bonus. Otherwise, you'd just be listening, as if to a radio. The physical element went for many years unheeded in films.'

Risking the wrath of Johnny Stompanato – Connery with Lana Turner, Another Time, Another Place *(1958)* ☆

Scotland's finest Irishman, sucking face for Walt Disney, in Darby O'Gill and the Little People, *1959* ☆

Years later, Connery was still extolling the virtues of Malmgren's teaching to *Empire* magazine, showing how profound an effect these exercises, and what he took from them, had on his overall career. 'If, for instance, you wanted to see a character who was all head and no body, it would be Cassius in *Julius Caesar*, the lean and hungry look they all talk about. He's just all-manipulating,

whereas Mark Antony is very much a weight person, charismatic. This usually starts with the body, because that's our first impression and it's what makes people respond or not. I won't even take a role until I work out the body techniques.'

When casting Sean Connery as James Bond just a few years later, producer Cubby Broccoli would famously describe the Scottish actor as walking with the grace and threat of a panther. Clearly, given the character he would be playing, this was no casual or natural gait.

While Connery was busy building a better model of actor, it was clear that the film industry of the day didn't really know what to do with him. Offers from Fox were being rejected, although Hollywood – or least what Hollywood had to offer in terms of world stardom – was still the goal. Connery's first significant role in a movie came in 1958 when he was loaned out from Fox to Paramount, to star opposite Lana Turner as a BBC war correspondent in *Another Time, Another Place*. Turner had personally selected Connery as her British leading man (even though he dies in the first twenty minutes), a fact that led to notable tensions during production, when her lover, noted gangster Johnny Stompanato, became jealous of her new romantic lead. Stompanato's abuse of Turner and his disruption of the set led to his being banned from the studio. He headed back to the States, but would reappear in a most unwelcome manner in Connery's life on his first visit to Hollywood.

Connery was later typically candid about the movie that could have launched him in the States: 'One's intuitive senses were saying that the director is an idiot. I'd no influence or authority at the time, so my protests went unheeded. But at least I learned

from it.' The film was both a commercial and critical disaster, but, with the benefit of hindsight, the review in the *Sunday Express* at least nowadays provides some pleasure, describing Connery as 'a newcomer to films who will not, I guess, grow old in the industry'.

Connery later said of the film, 'I acted with Lana Turner in *Another Time, Another Place* – which it should have been.'

Walt Disney, however, liked what he saw. Enough to cast Connery as the lead in his live-action leprechaun romp, *Darby O'Gill and the Little People*. This was Connery's biggest and most prestigious movie role to date. It also afforded him the opportunity to record and release his one and only single. When asked by *Empire* magazine some thirty years later if he could remember the words to 'My Pretty Irish Girl', Connery laughed, cleared his throat and started to sing: '"She's my dear/My darling one/My smiling and beguiling one/Dah dah de dah/Dah dah dah dah/ My Pretty Irish Girl" – God, I haven't even thought about that for years. And, you know, me and [co-star] Janet Munro were making that single for Disney and they suddenly announced there'd be a B-side, so Janet went out to get a bottle of vodka, came back and we had two very large vodkas, and they just gave us the sheet.' Remarkably, Connery also remembered the words to that B-side, 'The Bally McQuilty Band',

Many felt he should have been wearing the loincloth, but instead Connery played a rare bad guy role in Tarzan's Greatest Adventure *(1959)* ☆

although, unlike the film, neither song was a hit.

More importantly, *Darby O'Gill* was the film that first brought Sean Connery to Hollywood. 'I didn't realize that on the plane all the food and drink were free,' he said of the flight over. 'It took me ages to order something.'

Once in town to begin filming, Connery found that all was not well. Lana Turner's daughter Cheryl Crane had stabbed and killed Johnny Stompanato after another in a series of increasingly violent domestic arguments. It was the scandal that Connery blew into town with. The next day at his hotel the actor received an anonymous phone call, advising him to get out of town. Word had it that Stompanato had been convinced Turner had had an affair with Connery, and his cohorts were out to settle some scores.

'My problem was that I owed my hotel $600,' said Connery, 'and I was in the middle of a big row with the studio. But I got out and went to a hotel in the San Fernando Valley where I lay low. Nothing did happen, but it was scary as hell for a while.'

Still picking up the £120 a week from Fox, Connery had yet to make a Fox film. However, eager to groom their potential new star during his stay in Hollywood, Fox invited him to enrol in their charm school; Connery turned them down flat. He also turned down potentially lucrative offers to star in American TV shows such as *Maverick* and *Wyatt Earp*. 'They might have earned me a fortune, but they'd have finished me as an actor.'

Connery knew his goal wasn't to be achieved in weekly television, but given such career-minded wisdom, it's a surprise that he readily agreed to Fox's next move, loaning him out once again to appear in *Tarzan's Greatest Adventure*. Given that his minor role saw him squarely back in the muscle department, one can only imagine that Connery signed up for this one – generally considered to be around the twenty-third best Tarzan film ever made! – as an excuse to visit Kenya and pick up some cash.

Back in England, the actor was once again going through the motions in motion pictures, a medium that still seemed uncertain what to do with him, and totally unaware of what it had on its hands.

In 1961, *The Frightened City* provided Connery with his biggest role to date, opposite the likes of Herbert Lom and Alfred Marks. Set in London's Soho, Connery starred as an Irish gangster named Paddy Damion.

This was followed by a comic turn, alongside Alfred Lynch in *On the Fiddle*, with Connery effectively charming as Pedlar Pascoe, desperately trying to avoid active service in World War II. For the first time, Connery received top billing, but still stardom seemed as far away as ever. *Woman*

Getting tough on the streets of Soho in The Frightened City *(1961)* ☆

magazine at the time hit the nail on the proverbial: 'It's a real mystery to me why no film company has built Sean Connery into a great international star. He reminded me of Clark Gable. He has the same rare mixture of handsome virility, sweetness and warmth.'

If the movies were proving a disappointment to Connery, he was more than compensated by his work on both television and the stage. The legacy of *Requiem for a Heavyweight*, and the attendant press coverage of starring opposite Lana Turner and working for Walt Disney, meant that Connery was in constant demand on the British box. In 1958, he appeared in a prestigious production of *Women in Love* for ITV, working again for the independent company the following June in *The Square Ring*. Here, Connery once more played a boxer, in a tense

dressing-room-set drama, also featuring a young Alan Bates.

That November, again for ITV, the Scot took on the not inconsiderable role of John Proctor in a TV adaptation of Arthur Miller's *The Crucible*, turning in a performance that was met with considerable critical acclaim.

Two months later, at the start of the decade that he would definitely help to swing, Connery was back at the BBC for Jean Anouilh's *Colombe* and, more importantly, taking a prominent role in that corporation's epic serialization of Shakespeare's history plays. Presented under the banner title of *An Age of Kings*, Connery was cast as Hotspur opposite his friend Robert Hardy's Prince Hal in the first four of twelve episodes (effectively comprising *Henry IV*). Interviewed in the *Radio Times*, Connery commented that 'The most gratifying thing about

Lightening up and doing the dishes: On the Fiddle *(1961)* ☆

the series has been the warm response to Shakespeare by people who would not normally go five yards to see one of his plays.'

Secret-agent training came that autumn in the role of international spy Innes Corrie in the BBC thriller *Without the Grail*. Corrie, a James Bond precursor in many ways, was saddled with the less than glamorous task of investigating Michael Hordern's somewhat unbalanced tea baron.

This regular, and increasingly acclaimed TV work, was balanced for the actor by constant returns to the theatre, although he was not always successful in landing the roles he wanted. In his autobiography, playwright John Osborne remembers turning Connery down for a role in his 1959 production, *The World of Paul Slickey*. 'I made a monumental misjudgement by dismissing Sean Connery, who turned up one morning looking like my prejudiced idea of a Rank contract actor.'

In 1959, Connery returned to Edinburgh to appear opposite Sybil Thorndike in a production of *The Sea Shell*, and then re-emerged at the Oxford Playhouse, opposite Diane Cilento once again, in Pirandello's *Naked*. By this time, Cilento's first marriage was faltering and her relationship with Sean Connery was blossoming. Her career as an actress was also taking off, peaking with her Oscar-nominated appearance opposite Albert Finney in *Tom Jones* in 1963. 'We did not fall in love for a year or more after our first meeting,' the actress once recalled of Connery. 'He was not nearly as attractive in those days.'

Back on television, Sean Connery was becoming an increasingly familiar face. In late 1960, he could be seen in both the one-act drama *Riders to the Sea*, and alongside Robert Shaw in the TV dramatization of that actor's first novel, *The Pet*. The two tough-guy actors starred as British airmen, shot down over Germany during World War II and held captive by one of the locals. (The two soon became firm friends and would act together again

*Taking time out with
Turner, 1958 ☆*

in 1963's Bond thriller *From Russia With Love* and 1976's medieval thriller *Robin and Marian*.)

The year 1961 saw Sean Connery, complete with blond curly wig, gracing the cover of the *Radio Times* as Alexander the Great in the TV adaptation of Terence Rattigan's *Adventure Story*. Tellingly, the review of the show in *The Times* picked up not only on Connery's potential abilities, but also on the technicalities of Connery's approach to the craft of acting. 'Certain inflections and swift deliberations of gesture at times made one feel that the part had found the young Olivier it needs.'

The director of *Adventure Story*, Rudolph Cartier, was so impressed with the Scot's Greek that he immediately cast him as the romantic lead in his next production, *Anna Karenina*, starring Claire Bloom. It was to prove a lucky role for Connery, given that it was seen by a producer named Harry Saltzman.

Tommy Connery had now spent around a decade constructing Sean Connery. He began by shaping his body, altering and developing his physique for show. He then removed himself from the world he had known, the world of the stair and the milk round, into a world that was undoubtedly alien to all those he knew back home, that of the theatre. And while he never in any way denied his past – indeed his steadfast allegiance to his accent has always been seen as a statement of pride – he clearly wanted much more than it could offer him. He read what he needed to know, and more. Watched all that he could, and took from it what he deemed useful. He used endless hours of tape recordings to develop his voice. He studied movement to make his gestures an essential element of all that he wanted to communicate in any role. He wanted to be a movie star and yet, despite critical acclaim on TV, and the power of Hollywood's Twentieth Century–Fox behind him, he still wasn't one.

The problem was that this self-made man was a new kind of actor. He needed a new kind of movie. A new kind of character. He found him in the form of a British spy named after an American birdwatcher. The name was Bond. James Bond.

2. The Classless Hero

Today, James Bond is a cliché. The movies, while still hugely entertaining, have become a series of oft-repeated moments that audiences all too willingly wait to savour – Bond ordering his Martini, shaken not stirred, as ever, his inevitable appearance in a casino, his flirting with Moneypenny, the pun-heavy Bond-girl names – from Pussy Galore to Xenia Onatopp – the bigger-and-better-than last-time stunts. Indeed, watching a new actor assume the mantle of the world's most famous secret agent is akin to evaluating someone's Hamlet – just as you wait for 'To be, or not to be', so you judge the actor by his delivery of 'The name's Bond. James Bond.'

Back in 1962, however, James Bond was a breath of cinematic fresh air. British life post-World War II was a black-and-white world. Rationing was still in everyone's recent memory, and movies were making huge thematic breakthroughs with the so-called kitchen-sink dramas, such as *Saturday Night and Sunday Morning* and *Room at the Top*. The alternative was the recently launched *Carry On* series, a low-brow series of seaside postcards on celluloid. American cinema was,

Ian Fleming comes face to face with his most famous creation, on the beach in Jamaica, filming Dr No *(1962)* ☆

meanwhile, fairly moribund. The stars and sex symbols of Hollywood's golden age were now long past their prime, while of the new breed who had emerged to replace them, James Dean was already dead, and Brando was rapidly losing the plot.

When Bond arrived, he arrived in Technicolor, with an electric guitar playing his theme, surrounded by a bevy of beautiful women, in impossibly glamorous locations, not some studio-bound mock-up. Emerging as he did concurrently with the Beatles, James Bond helped introduce Britain, and subsequently the world, to the sixties.

Canadian producer Harry Saltzman had been largely responsible for the kitchen-sink dramas that dominated British cinema in the late 1950s, early 1960s. Forming Woodfall Films with writer John Osborne and director Tony Richardson, he had a hand in *Look Back in Anger*, *The Entertainer* and *Saturday Night and Sunday Morning*. But Saltzman quickly realized there was only so much grim reality that any paying cinema-goer could take; what they really wanted was not a reminder of life, but an escape from it. And so he began his pursuit of Ian Fleming's master spy.

The Eton-educated Fleming had spent the war years working in naval intelligence, rising to the rank of commander, the same rank he would bestow on his fictional creation. In 1953, sitting in his house, named Goldeneye, in Jamaica, Fleming conceived of a series of adventures involving a British Secret Service agent who would travel the world with a licence to kill on behalf of his country. The number he was assigned was 007; his name Fleming took from a book on West Indian birds, written by an ornithologist called James Bond.

The result was *Casino Royale*, an instant best-seller. Having caught the public's imagination, Fleming continued to deliver a new Bond adventure just about every year, eventually being able to number US President John F. Kennedy among his loyal readership.

Shortly after publication of that first book, Fleming sold the screen rights to an American producer and James Bond made his first appearance on American television in the form of actor Barry Nelson. Nelson's Americanized 'Jimmy' Bond bore little resemblance to Fleming's ultra British hero, and subsequently the one-off show was not deemed a success. So while the books continued to sell, there was little interest in bringing Bond back to the screen.

In 1958, director Kevin McClory approached Fleming with the idea of making an original Bond movie. The project was soon abandoned, but *Longitude 78 West*, the script they developed together, and which Fleming later adapted into the novel *Thunderball*, has proved to be a continuing source of legal action and frustration for Bond's

No one remembers Bond in shorts, but everyone remembers Ursula Andress in that bikini *– Dr No (1962)* ☆

One last turn in the trenches before becoming Bond: Sean Connery's brief appearance in the star-heavy The Longest Day *(1962)* ☆

eventual producers right up to the present day. In 1960, Saltzman optioned all of Fleming's Bond titles, with the exception of the already sold *Casino Royale*, for a period of six months, for a remarkable fee of $50,000.

Albert Broccoli's family hold the distinction of having introduced a vegetable to the world. Albert, 'Cubby' to his friends, had in his day – like Sean Connery – worked for a coffin maker. He'd subsequently worked as an agent and now he was a film producer, having formed Warwick Films, and produced the run-of-the-mill World War II adventure *The Cockleshell Heroes*.

Broccoli also believed that what the public really wanted now was escapism and he too saw Fleming's

spy as the perfect opportunity to provide just that, but when he looked into optioning the books from Fleming he saw that another producer, Harry Saltzman, had already done so. A mutual friend put them in touch with each other and when Harry met Cubby, they decided to go into business together, and formed Eon Productions.

They quickly chose *Dr No* – originally derived from a script Fleming had written for a potential TV series named *Commander Jamaica* – to be their first James Bond film. All they needed was a studio to back them, and an actor to play the part.

Columbia pictures were interested at first, provided the Eon boys could get Cary Grant to play Bond. Grant read the script and agreed to play the part, but would not commit himself to a series of Bonds, and right from the beginning Saltzman and Broccoli intended to develop 007 into a franchise, little realizing it would become the longest-running, most profitable franchise in movie history.

So Grant was out, as was James Mason, who said he'd do two, but no more. Fleming himself favoured his friend David Niven, a name that cropped up in the newspapers, which were awash with speculation and rumour as to who could or should play Fleming's master spy. The list of possibilities ran from Peter Finch, Richard Burton, Rex Harrison and Trevor Howard to relative newcomers like Patrick McGoohan and Roger Moore. A poll in the *Daily Express* listed the top ten choices to play Bond, among them an actor named Sean Connery, who had recently scored on television in *Anna Karenina*.

Broccoli was more and more convinced that the part of James Bond should be played by a relative unknown. As the character emerged, so would the actor, for ever linking the two in the public's eye.

Aware of the publicity the movie was already generating, Bud Ornstein, the head of United Artists' London office, decided to come on board. The American office agreed, imposing a strict budget of $1 million.

Terence Young was hired as director. As with the casting of the central character, deciding on Young had not been an easy choice for Eon, who again wanted someone who would commit to a string of movies, not just the one. Bryan Forbes passed on it, while Guy Hamilton (who would later direct *Goldfinger*) tentatively agreed, then backed away. Young signed up and quickly nominated Sean Connery for the role. He had, of course, directed the young Scot in *Action of the Tiger*. 'He has a good voice, and more importantly, splendid presence,' the director said, 'and a quality that I have seen in only one man previously: Clark Gable.'

While the casting of James Bond was running rampant with speculation, Sean Connery was busy severing his ties with Twentieth Century Fox. After nearly four years, he had yet to make a single movie for them, and he was more than a little annoyed with having to ask their permission every time he wanted to accept another screen offer. Having failed to work out what to do with this burly, stubborn, opinionated man with the strange accent, the American film company was happy to let him go. As a parting gesture he appeared in their World War II epic *The Longest Day*, but then again, so did everyone else, boasting an all-star cast that included the likes of John Wayne, Robert Mitchum, Henry Fonda, Richard Burton and more.

He was now once again a free agent and, after some impressive TV work, he was an actor with a growing reputation.

Still, Eon weren't convinced. At Young's urging, Saltzman screened *On the Fiddle* in London, while over in Los Angeles, Broccoli viewed *Darby O'Gill and the Little People*. Both were impressed with Connery, but the deciding vote unexpectedly lay with Broccoli's wife Dana, who upon viewing the Scot in his Disney debut proclaimed him to be a 'very sexy guy'.

Connery was promptly called into their offices in London's South Audley Street. Young telephoned the actor beforehand and suggested he wear his one and only suit to impress the producers, but, ever wilful, Connery showed up in casual, even scruffy, informal attire. The clothes may have been casual, but his approach to the meeting was anything but.

Connery was instantly assertive, taking charge, banging his fist on the table to emphasize his points, moving around the room to command the attention of everyone in attendance. When the producers mentioned the possibility of a screen test, Connery flatly refused, telling them they could take him or leave him on the strength of what they'd seen. It was a one-off offer, in retrospect, one of the most fateful in movie history.

'He was wearing baggy, unpressed trousers, a brown shirt without a tie and suede shoes,' said Broccoli, 'and he thumped and pounded the desk and told us what he wanted. I think that's what impressed us – the fact that he'd got balls.'

Having laid his cards on the table, Connery left the meeting. Both Saltzman and Broccoli moved to the window to watch the actor walk away in the street below. Both were struck by the way he moved, the gracefulness he brought to his size, the sense of aggression they had witnessed themselves, tempered with this cat-like gait, easy-moving, but always with the threat of danger lurking underneath. Broccoli would later say that it was this walk away that secured the role for Connery.

'We watched him bounce across the road like he was Superman, and Harry and I believed we had to go along with him no matter what anyone else said.'

Connery himself would later reveal that the man he had very deliberately shown them in that room was not a former milkman from Edinburgh, but the man James Bond could be.

'I used strong and commanding movements,' the Yat Malmgren-trained actor later explained. 'Not with weight, but to show how Bond is always in control of a scene.'

Saltzman and Broccoli were convinced they'd found their man, even if during negotiating his contract, he did decide to pop over to Canada at short notice for a television version of *Macbeth*. Connery agreed to sign on for five movies, with the proviso that he be allowed to make one non-Bond movie a year in between. 'The difference with this guy,' said Broccoli about Connery, 'is the difference

That look, that sneer, that hairpiece – a legend is born ☆

between a still photograph and film. When he starts to move, he comes alive.'

For his first outing as 007, he was paid what he thought then to be the princely sum of £6,000. He would not always think of his producers as such generous men.

On 3 November 1961, it was announced to the world that Sean Connery would be James Bond. Or, indeed, that James Bond would be Sean Connery. 'It was a bit of a joke around town that I was chosen for Bond. The character is not really me, after all.'

Having landed the most coveted role in contemporary cinema, Sean Connery then had to set about bringing the character to life. 'I had to start playing Bond from scratch – not even Ian Fleming knew much about Bond at this time.' This was true, as Fleming had never wanted Bond to be seen as a full, rounded character, but more as a cipher, a deliberately mysterious figure, whose private life was for the most part his own, moving from one adventure to another, one woman to another. There was also work to be done on Connery physically. Diane Cilento, whose relationship with the actor was still largely under wraps as she awaited her divorce, worked with him, convinced this was the big break he'd been waiting for. Indeed, at the time she was more convinced than Connery, who when Joan Collins and husband Anthony Newley asked him at a casual meeting

what he was working on next, reportedly replied, 'It'll be just another job, then I'll be waiting for the phone to ring again as usual.'

Terence Young, meanwhile, worked on the visual side. First up, was the issue of hair. Or lack of it. Connery already displayed a significant receding hairline, and this was one of the producers' primary concerns. The actor playing Eton-educated Commander Bond could be working class, he could be from Scotland, but he couldn't be bald. A toupée was procured for Connery's first – and all subsequent – appearances as 007.

Next came the grooming. Terence Young took Connery to his tailor, shirt and shoe maker to provide him with a wardrobe somewhere beyond the Army & Navy corduroy trousers the actor favoured. In addition, he introduced him to the rarefied atmosphere of the St James Club and took him to the best restaurants in Mayfair, where the two men discussed what a certain secret agent might order from the various menus.

To be the spy, Connery knew he had to again work on the physical aspects of the role, taking the time to feel comfortable in the clothing that Bond would undoubtedly wear.

Ian Fleming had provided the hanger, Terence Young had provided the clothes, and now Sean Connery had to find out what he brought to Bond. Alongside his sexual charisma and physical presence, what Connery really brought to the role was a certain classlessness that hadn't really existed in Britain before the 1960s. While Bond as written in the novels was a man of privilege, born of his education and naval rank, Connery, in both his voice and his mannerisms, showed little or no respect for that world. Yes, he was still a man who you believed could rate a '53 Dom Perignon over a '57, but he clearly wasn't ruled by that knowledge. He was a sensualist, a man who pleased himself first and foremost and damn the consequences. What Fleming envisaged as an upper-class gentleman killer, Connery made into a classless hero, a man who made his own rules and walked in a world of his own creating. A key element in portraying this, and one that Connery more than anyone else brought to the part, was humour. Bond could kill a man or bed a babe and still find time to deliver an appropriate pun, accompanied by a sly smirk. It's a mannerism that has been aped by countless screen figures since from Dirty Harry to Freddy Kruger and beyond. But Connery, quite rightly, lays claim to doing it first.

The other thing of course was the accent – but that was there to stay. 'I talked a lot to the author of the Bond novels, Ian Fleming, and to the director Terence Young about the physical aspect, and also about my accent. I've always had a terrible fight to get work in Britain on account of my Edinburgh accent. And I still haven't lost it completely. I won't – because I don't think it's right to lose it.'

In January 1962, Sean Connery flew to Jamaica to begin filming on *Dr No*, the film that would make James Bond an icon and Sean Connery a star. The first scene shot was Bond's arrival at the local airport.

Essentially working on a low-budget movie, far away from home, both star and director were a little uncertain. 'There were times when Terence and I were on location and both thinking, '"What on earth have we here? Will anyone want to watch?"'

Whatever fears Young had were quickly assuaged, as the director later recalled. 'I think he really said, "This is my chance. I've made a lot of unsuccessful pictures and this is the chance for me." After we'd been working together for a week I just knew that it was going to click, because he was really interested, he was really trying.'

During his stay on the island, Connery met Fleming's neighbour Noël Coward. Connery later recalled the encounter: 'I remember when I and Chris Blackwell were out in Jamaica, hanging out in all the music clubs, and we were filming one night in the bauxite mines. And we came out covered in red dust. And we were due to go to Noël's for dinner. So we turned up two hours late, covered in filth. And there is Noël in a plum dinner jacket, bow tie, long cigarette holder and he's playing the piano, accompanying himself on his own LP of his act live at Las Vegas. He never batted an eyelid. "Come in, dear boys," he said and we went and had a wash and he carried on playing right to the end of the LP, waiting for us, and when he was ready, he would start dinner.'

There was someone else Connery met on the Jamaica part of the shoot, a young actress named Ursula Andress. When she first emerged from the ocean, bearing only a white bikini, a large knife and the smirk-inducing name of Honey Ryder, she instantly provided the archetype for just about every actress who would ever be cast opposite 007 (even if her accent was too heavy and she had to be dubbed by another actress).

Filming was completed back at Pinewood studios just outside London.

After filming in the glamorous locales of Jamaica, after coolly saving the world from the mad scientist figure of Dr No on the sound stages of Pinewood, after picking up the largest pay cheque of his career and faced with the prospect of a role that could very well see him made for life, Sean Connery decided it was time to repair to a dwelling that well befitted his new-found and impending status. So he moved to… Acton.

For those who have never had the pleasure and privilege of visiting this particular London suburb, all you need to know is it wasn't the kind of place you usually found movie stars. But it was the kind of place where a canny Scot could pick up a housing bargain, and Connery certainly did that when he purchased an ex-convent for £9,000 in April 1962. Diane Cilento was pregnant, and they needed what would become, after her divorce, a family home. Acacia House, as it was known, was situated in a cul-de-sac just off Acton High Street, and became just that.

Whilst awaiting the release of the first Bond adventure later that year, Connery took time to go back in to the theatre and star in a summer production of *Judith*.

Cilento's divorce was due in October, the same month that *Dr No* was to premiere. At first, Saltzman and Broccoli were worried about their movie. The American arm of United Artists had viewed it – largely with disdain – and were planning only a nominal release in the States, a factor that, financially, could have put the future franchise to rest even before it had begun.

Nonetheless, British hopes were high and they went ahead with a star-studded premiere in London's Leicester Square on the evening of 6 October 1962.

The critics may have been divided, but the audiences came in droves, making *Dr No* the second highest earning film in Britain in 1962.

In between filming his first Bond and the onslaught of its release, Connery briefly returned to the stage for the 1962 production of Judith *(with Ruth Meyers in the title role) at Her Majesty's Theatre, London* ☆

With second Bond girl Daniela Bianchi, in From Russia With Love *(1963)* ☆

What they were responding to was a kind of cinema they hadn't seen before. Glamorous locations and exotic characters at that time seemed to be the province of American movies, not indigenous to the United Kingdom at all. In Connery, they had someone who could be a truly international movie star, and in Bond they found a hero unlike any other. Here was a man who sold sex and sadism and made it all palatable with Connery's sense of satire. He bedded women with ease, he killed villains with ease and a smirk. He was best defined by that word that truly came into its own in the 1960s – *modern*. James Bond was just incredibly modern, able, it appeared, to move effortlessly through a society still profoundly divided by a class system, bound by his own personal sense of self, not amoral as such, but not tied down to ancient notions of morality. He was the sensualist Connery had imagined, ruthless with a gun and by all appearances lethal in another way with women. Bond lived life to the full, even before the term 'permissive society' had been coined. The 1960s had begun.

While James Bond was ushering in a new age of sexual liberation, Sean Connery was doing the decent thing and marrying his pregnant girlfriend. Despite the attendant publicity from the launch of *Dr No*, Connery was determined to keep his private life just that, and was well aware that the notion of

James Bond getting married would have resulted in a media zoo. Consequently, he and Cilento decamped to Gibraltar and were married at the local registry office. They honeymooned in Spain, a country that instantly appealed to Connery. Their son Jason was born in Rome on 12 January 1963.

Having seen *Dr No*'s amazing success in Britain, where it quickly made back its $1 million budget and went into profit, the American arm of United Artists revised their plans for releasing the film – originally they planned to put it out on a double bill with a Jerry Lewis vehicle – and found themselves with a major hit on their hands, confirming James Bond as a worldwide phenomenon.

Everyone was eager for a follow-up and *From Russia With Love* was chosen. The budget this time around was nearly $2 million and Connery's own fee rose considerably. Pre-publicity for the film saw the press covering a story about how a tuxedo-clad Sean Connery, draping three gorgeous starlets on his arm, had picked up £10,000 in a casino in northern Italy using a system Ian Fleming had devised for Bond. The line between Connery the actor and Bond the icon was blurring noticeably.

From Russia With Love began filming at Pinewood Studios in April of 1963, later taking in locations in Turkey, Spain and Scotland (with Scotland standing in for Turkey when the company was forced to decamp under the threat of an imminent political revolution). Terence Young was once again calling the shots, while Connery was provided with £1,000-worth of Savile Row's finest.

The Bond formula was also being actively developed. At Saltzman's suggestion, a pre-credit action sequence was added, something that was to become a major staple of all subsequent Bond films. Desmond Llewelyn made his first appearance as the gadget man (although he was billed as 'Boothroyd', not 'Q'), supplying 007 with a multi-purpose briefcase, a tame tool in comparison with the ones that Bond would later receive. John Barry, whose distinctive scores came to be a key element in the Bonds, came on board, while Italian actress Daniela Bianchi became the second of what were to become known as the Bond Girls (and the second one to have her dialogue dubbed by another actress). Lotte Lenya as the lethally booted Rosa Klebb and Robert Shaw's dyed-blond assassin Red Grant joined Dr No in the gallery of Bond villains.

Such was the demand for Bond that the movie received its world premiere a mere two months after it had finished filming, on 10 October 1963.

Leicester Square was packed with thousands desperate to get a glimpse of their new-found hero. More than merely building on the success of *Dr No*, *From Russia With Love*, the most serious-minded of all the Bond movies, went on to become the highest grossing film in British cinema history. Its huge success was reflected in the US, where it earned a total of $24 million, a vast amount for the day.

Sean Connery, who less than eighteen months before, was struggling to find TV work, was now the number-one box-office star on the planet. Not that he was happy.

'Sean and I were in America just after the release of *From Russia With Love* in 1963,' Terence Young once recalled, 'and we sneaked out the side entrance of the airport. And there must have been seven or eight hundred people out there. There was an old lady there who came through the ring of cops wanting an autograph and I said, "Sean, sign the bloody thing." So Sean signed it and gave it to her, and she looked horrified. "No, no," she said, "I wanted James Bond." She looked at Sean and Sean sort of crumpled. It suddenly occurred to him that he was no longer a human being, he was a symbol.'

Connery may have had his doubts about being consumed by his character, but Broccoli and Saltzman had no such worries. They simply knew that the public wanted Bond; along with the Beatles, James Bond was leading a British invasion of the world and everyone wanted more, more, more of it all.

The third Bond movie, *Goldfinger*, began filming in March 1964. Connery had secured himself a significantly higher pay day of £50,000 plus a percentage of the profits, but Terence Young had not been as successful in attempting to get the Eon producers to renegotiate his terms, and had left the movie during pre-production. Similarly, writer Paul Dehn had been drafted in to replace regular screenwriter Richard Maibaum.

The image of the Bond girl was subtly redefined in the form of the splendidly named Pussy Galore, who was more than a match for Bond out of the bedroom, played to perfection by Honor Blackman, already a big star in Britain due to her role as Cathy Gale in TV's *The Avengers*. Gert Frobe was cast as the villainous Goldfinger and the small but deadly Harold Sakata stole the show as the lethal Oddjob.

With a budget of £2.9 million, *Goldfinger* upped the stakes for Bond movies, blessed as it was with Ken Adam's superb set design and such ultra-cool gadgets as the classic ejector seat Aston Martin, for many still Bond's greatest accessory. More than anything, Connery had got to the point where his performance as Bond appeared effortless, an assured, beguiling mix of urbanity and self-mockery, relaxed, poised and perfect. Audiences readily agreed, taking the Bond bandwagon

to greater heights than ever before, with *Goldfinger* becoming the fastest earning movie in film history, rounding out with a astonishing box-office total of nearly $55 million. The soundtrack album – only a part of the huge merchandising operation based around Bond, which Connery saw no part of – proved so successful, that it knocked the Beatles off the top spot in the album charts. Even the Queen Mother liked it, telling Connery it was the best film she'd ever seen.

At the time of *Goldfinger*'s release Sean Connery was receiving 1,500 fan letters a week, yet he was still shocked by the amazing turnout when he attended the French premiere in Paris, making his entrance along the Champs Elysées in Bond's Aston Martin, accompanied by six gold-wearing, scooter-driving starlets. One fan jumped the barricades and hurled herself into the Aston, landing squarely on her hero's lap.

Ian Fleming, however, never got to see it. He died of a fatal heart attack one month before the film's premiere. Connery heard of the news while on an Italian golf course with Rex Harrison. Robert Shaw had introduced him to the game during the filming of *From Russia With Love* and Connery had quickly fallen in love with what remains a lifetime passion. In memory of Fleming, he went back out on the course and played a further eighteen holes. It seemed the thing to do.

Bond takes a breather –
relaxing on location:
Goldfinger *(1964)* ☆

James Bond had made Sean Connery, but the actor was beginning to find himself overwhelmed by the role. As his frustration with the character rose, so did his antipathy towards his producers, whom he saw as earning vast fortunes off the back of his hard work. This, coupled with a punishing work rate as he struggled to fit in other movies between his Bond stints, began to take its toll on his marriage to Cilento. In March of 1965, he moved out of their house in Acton, for what was to be only a temporary separation, although it did scupper their plans to make the film *Big Country, Big Man* together in Australia, later that year.

Shortly after, with Bondmania increasing, Connery once again found himself ensconced at Pinewood, now working on *Thunderball*. Kevin McClory had threatened to make his own version of the story he co-owned the rights to, with Richard Burton apparently interested in playing 007. 'I think he must be out of his mind,' was Connery's response. 'It would be like putting his head on a chopping board. Whatever he did couldn't make the films more successful than they are.'

Broccoli and Saltzman were eager to protect their golden goose, and resolved the rights issues swiftly, giving Kevin McClory a producing credit on the movie.

Although Connery was fiercely protective of his private life, the media cavalcade that surrounded

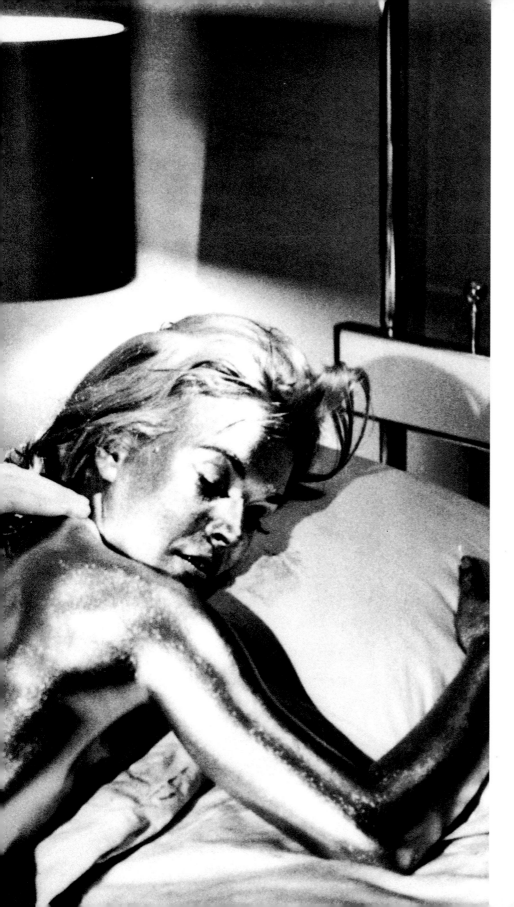

the filming of *Thunderball* was intense, and every move he or Cilento made was monitored, reported, commented on, digested and dismissed in favour of the next bulletin. When the James Bond machine – Terence Young back in place – headed to the Bahamas for location and underwater work, the press went with them.

It was flashbulbs a go-go at the airport on the island of Nassau in April when Cilento flew out to join the husband she was apparently estranged from. They stayed on the aptly named Love Beach, hiding out from the incessant glare of the world's paparazzi. For once, and much to his displeasure, Connery's off-screen life was attracting as much attention as James Bond's cinematic one.

Perhaps the problems in the marriage came from the way in which Connery's career seemed to be eclipsing Cilento's. It was certainly something that had been on her mind. 'I am through the other side of being Mrs James Bond,' she said, 'and although it still happens, it cannot upset me any longer. Sean and I have our lives to lead in our own way. Strangely enough, I am not too ambitious any more, I am not caught up. I have my children and my home and I shall work when it is right and only then. But we are not going to let ourselves be merchandized.'

For the most part, the actor kept away from the press. But one interview he agreed to do, with

Playboy magazine, has continued to haunt him throughout his career. During the interview, speaking more from the perspective of Bond rather than himself, Connery stated, 'It's not the worst thing to slap a woman now and then.' Still defending that line more than twenty years later – after it had resurfaced in the press more than once – Connery explained what he meant. 'I'm talking about a slap on the face and that you could do much, much worse damage to a woman, or a man, by totally demoralizing them, by taking away their whole identity. I'm saying that if one of the couple is intent on having a physical confrontation, then it's impossible for it to be avoided. It's emotional, it's passion. And passion lacks thinking. Therefore, it will explode.'

The Bond machine had become unstoppable. The accountants worked out that for every hour of the day, each and every day, the three previous movies were earning $1,000. Everyone was getting rich, in Connery's opinion some more than others. During the filming of *Thunderball*, he was not a happy man. His personal problems aside, his relationship with Broccoli and Saltzman was rapidly deteriorating. While he was well compensated, he felt that his part in the success of all the films was being denigrated. His producers clearly thought that the character, not the actor, had made the movies the huge hits they were. He felt he should be an equal partner in Eon, sharing the rewards he saw coming their way as a direct result of his performance. Broccoli, at least, was still convinced that Bond was the star and always would be.

Connery had two more Bonds left to go according to his contract, but during the difficult shoot of *Thunderball*, forty per cent of which takes place under water, he was already making his discontent known.

While the actor may have been unhappy, the public were delighted with the fourth James Bond film. The budget may now have risen to $5.5 million but it more than paid off at the box office, where *Thunderball* went on to become the highest grossing Bond to date. Some cinemas in America were forced to stay open for twenty-four hours a day to accommodate audiences hungry for more of their favourite superspy's adventures – $63 million was rapidly registered in US ticket sales alone. Sean Connery was on the cover of *Life* magazine, even though many readers simply thought it was a picture of James Bond.

Away from Bond-age Connery was struggling to establish himself as an actor of considerable range, working with such acclaimed directors as Alfred Hitchcock and Sidney Lumet. More and more, the thought of coming back to yet another increasingly exotic and gadget-heavy spy adventure was losing

PREVIOUS PAGE *Bond offers unnecessary neck massage to golden girl Shirley Eaton: Goldfinger (1964)* ☆

RIGHT *Prepare to dive – Connery with Bond girls Claudine Auger and Martine Beswick, on location for Thunderball, April 1965* ☆

Taking to the air in an autogyro made for one, in You Only Live Twice *(1967)* ☆

its appeal. 'At this point,' he said, 'there is no more I can get out of Bond as an actor. All one really needs is the constitution of a rugby player to get through nineteen weeks of swimming, slugging and necking.'

Spurred on by the amazing financial success of the Bond films, the American producer, Charles Feldman, who owned the rights to *Casino Royale*, planned to make a rival movie and propositioned Connery, asking him what it would take to get the Scot to defect. A cool million was what he wanted. Feldman passed, and eventually ended up with a huge, overpriced, underwhelming parody of the whole genre, that did little at the box office, despite combining the talents of Peter Sellers, David Niven, Orson Welles and Woody Allen.

Never a company to rest on its receipts, Eon was already moving ahead with Bond's next official adventure. *You Only Live Twice* would see pussy-loving arch-enemy Ernst Blofeld finally revealed on camera in the form of a scarred Donald Pleasence (the credits at the end of *From Russia With Love* had cryptically shown Blofeld as being played by '?'), Bondmania shoot through the roof on location in Japan, Ken Adam literally take the roof off a volcano in his beautifully excessive designs for the film (a set which cost $1 million, the entire budget of *Dr No*) and Sean Connery reach the end of his tether by the end of filming. To be honest, Connery had reached the end of his tether even before he started. 'I'm finished,' he said before scene one was in the can. 'Bond's been good to me, but I've done my bit. I'm out.'

By the time filming began on what looked likely to be Sean Connery's farewell to Her Majesty's Secret Service, he was reunited with his wife, and had traded in his house in Acton for accommodation in both Putney and Spain. 'We have a marvellous house in Acton, in a wonderful situation – a cul-de-sac right by the park,' he explained in a TV interview. 'But there are some real headcases around. They just come up and sit on top of their cars, or knock on the door and say it would be marvellous if they could come in and have tea, or take some photographs, or stand on your wall. There's only one way to solve it, and that's not to be there.'

He may have been reconciled with his wife, but Connery was now most definitely estranged from his producers. He no longer spoke to Saltzman and his dealings with Broccoli were terse. The actor knew he was well paid for what he did, but felt increasingly uncomfortable about what he felt was exploitation.

'I am concerned about the money I earn from them,' he said, 'because I think I should get every penny I'm entitled to.' In other words, someone was earning from the $60-million a-year turnover that

Once more unto the casino – Bond trumps the villainous Adolfo Celi in Thunderball *(1965)* ☆

had sprung up in Bond merchandise, and it certainly wasn't the star of the films.

'I don't talk to the producers. It's been a fight since the beginning. If they'd had any sense of fairness, they could have made me a partner. It would have been beneficial for all. It could have been a very happy thing if they had been fair.'

Connery's worries about how much James Bond had subsumed his life were rapidly proved right when the production moved to Japan to shoot on location and the actor found himself experiencing scenes of public adulation on a Beatle-like level. 'I had no idea of that scale of reverence. It was around the same time as the Beatles,' he recalled in 1998. 'The difference, of course, was that there were four of them to kick it around and blame each other.'

Mr and Mrs Sean Connery arrived on location in Tokyo on 27 July 1966. En route, the actor had already been mobbed in Bangkok and Manila and, upon arrival, found himself giving a press conference for hundreds of journalists. He arrived to find said journalists unprepared for his casual attire and lack of hairpiece. The first one braved his potential wrath by enquiring, 'Why are you, Mr James Bond, dressed like that?'

'I'm here for your bloody convenience and I can dress any way I damn well want,' was the reply that set the tone for the rest of the conference, Connery silently noting how many of the journalists thought they were interviewing Bond and not the actor who played him.

The Connerys stayed at the Tokyo Hilton, where the paparazzi laid siege to the lobby. The local papers were full of such rivetingly captioned photos as 'Sean Connery walks into the lobby' and 'Sean Connery walks out of the lobby'. Some went further. 'They followed me into the ruddy toilet,' he complained at the time. 'Coming at me like a firing squad. I've never known it like this before. I knew Bond was popular, but this has been incredible.'

After the toilet incident, the production hired twelve bodyguards, who all turned up with cameras and began shooting yet more snaps of their idol. When the shoot located to the far more remote island of Kyushu, thousands of fans followed them.

TV journalist Alan Whicker was on hand to cover the making of the film for a BBC documentary. Diane Cilento explained her husband's situation to him. 'He's been pushed beyond normal limits because everywhere you go someone's following him or hanging out of a tree.'

Connery was also dissatisfied with the production's various delays and problems. He wanted time away from Bond, but *You Only Live Twice* kept him tied up for over six months. Delays continued into filming, where, for example, a Czech actor hired to play Blofeld was dropped weeks into shooting, and Donald Pleasence hired in his place. 'They wanted me for Blofeld in a hurry,' the actor later recalled. 'Because of the rush, most of my role was filmed at Pinewood so I did not see a great deal of Sean. But I was aware of what was going on. It was something of a turning point for him, because he came out and said he would not do another Bond movie; this was going to be the last. I did not discuss it with him at the time but I could tell it was a delicate issue. So I did my three weeks of intensive work, and took the money and ran, as it were.'

You Only Live Twice was, as was now par for the course, a huge hit. But Connery decided he'd had enough. He was walking away from guaranteed continual success. He was, in the world's eyes, James Bond. But, from day one, he had sought not to be.

3. The Anti-image

Sean Connery knew from the moment he was offered the role of James Bond that it could be a curse as well as a blessing. Having spent several years tied to Twentieth Century–Fox, doing little more for them than taking their money, but having to go cap in hand to them every time he wanted to accept another job of work, he was wary about any form of long-term commitment.

Broccoli and Saltzman wanted their James Bond to work exclusively for them, for the duration of the first six Bond films. Wisely, Connery insisted from the off that he be allowed to make one film between each of the Bonds. He instinctively knew the power of the character and its potential to subsume him. He also knew what the role could offer him in terms of allowing him to do the work he really wanted to do on screen. James Bond was a millstone and a golden opportunity all wrapped up in one. It was a good plan; unfortunately it didn't go quite the way Connery had hoped.

The public's clamouring for more Bond after the wildly successful release of *Dr No*, coupled with his marriage and the subsequent birth of his son, meant that Connery's first film after his first James Bond, was his second James Bond. The rapid release of this new adventure kept him firmly in the public eye as Her Majesty's finest.

Although critics generally agreed that his performance in *From Russia With Love* was stronger than that in *Dr No*, Connery drew little satisfaction from the plaudits – it simply meant he was becoming a better Bond, cementing what he already perceived to be a worrisome tie with his gun-toting on-screen alter ego.

Connery read the screenplay to *Woman of Straw* while on location in Turkey for *From Russia With Love*. Distracted by what was already a difficult,

troublesome shoot, he later admitted he never really gave the script his full attention, a mistake he said he would never make again (which sadly doesn't explain *Zardoz!*). What appealed to him, however, was the opportunity to get as far away from Bond as possible (here he had the opportunity to play a villain), the chance to star opposite his acting idol Ralph Richardson, and the premonition that a thriller starring himself and current Euro-sex bomb Gina Lollobrigida could be a hit at the box office, proving Sean Connery more than a one-trick pony. Connery played Anthony Richmond, a manipulative playboy out to murder his rich uncle and pin the murder on Ms Lollobrigida's rather good-looking nurse. Alfred Hitchcock – who was waiting in the wings for Connery – might have made something decent of such material, but the

PREVIOUS PAGE *Taking it to the top,* Connery excels in *Sidney Lumet's powerful* The Hill *(1965)* ☆

LEFT *Discussing psycho-sexual subtext with* Marnie *director Alfred Hitchcock (not even Cary Grant got to do that!)* ☆

RIGHT *With Tippi Hedren in* Marnie *(1964)* ☆

film proved to be a disappointment all round, although in later years Connery was quick to shoulder the blame. 'I wasn't all that thrilled with *Woman of Straw*,' he conceded, 'although the problems were my own. I'd been working non-stop since goodness knows when and trying to suggest rewrites while making another film, *From Russia With Love*. It was an experience, but I won't make that mistake again. When it was shot down, I wasn't entirely surprised.'

It was shortly before filming *Goldfinger* that Connery was approached by Alfred Hitchcock to star in his next film, *Marnie*. *Marnie* had long been touted as the film that would bring Hitchcock's greatest filmic blonde – Grace Kelly, by now Princess Grace of Monaco – back to the big screen. When the princess passed, the director decided to go ahead anyway with Tippi Hedren, the woman many saw as his platinum-coated replacement model. The offer was sent out to Sean Connery to play the role of Mark Rutland, the tycoon who finds the deeply troubled kleptomaniac *Marnie* and, with mysterious motives, agrees to marry her in an attempt to save her. 'I told him to send the script and that I'd let him know if I accepted his offer. He

said it was nonsense my asking to see a script; that Cary Grant had never asked to see a script. I told him I wasn't Cary Grant and I never took a role unless I knew what I had to do and say.'

The script duly arrived, Connery studied it and signed on for the role, his first back in Hollywood since *Darby O'Gill* five years before. As before, he took the simple approach – when the production put him up at the luxurious Chateau Marmont and supplied him with a driver, he opted to stay at the same low-rent hotel he had last time and drove himself to work every morning. Indeed, this low-key approach to his own burgeoning stardom so endeared him to the crew and technicians on the film, whose company he preferred to keep during the film's shoot, that they all chipped in and presented him with a $1,000 watch at the end of filming.

When later commenting on Hitchcock's directing, Connery explained he only experienced it twice. 'I had a tendency sometimes to speak too quickly, and he would say, "Just sneak in some dog's feet," which was his way of saying "Pause." The other was, I was opening my mouth, listening to somebody talking to me, and he said, "I don't think people are interested in your dental work."'

In its day *Marnie* was moderately well received by Hitchcock's public and critics alike, seen as a fairly involving melodrama with more than a dollop of Freudian cod-psychology. Viewed with the glory of hindsight of course, *Marnie* becomes a much more intriguing piece of work, with Hitchcock opting to fill his film to the brim with what appears to be unmistakably obvious back projection, and even more unrealistic painted backdrops, the result of which is to create an quasi-expressionistic world.

While the psychology displayed in the film comes wholesale from the generic textbooks that form Rutland's reading, the real psychology of the film lies firmly off camera. Hitchcock's latter-day reputation paints him as a man in love with the icy blondes he created, frustrated by his own portly physicality but more than willing to exploit his own fantasies, desires and fetishes via his movies. As such, Tippi Hedren was very much his attempt to create a new Grace Kelly, to replace the woman he lost with a woman he could attempt to have. Indeed, legend has it that, already having made her a star in his previous production, *The Birds*, he propositioned the actress in her trailer during filming, and when rebuked, he set out to destroy her career, some say even to the point where he lost interest in *Marnie* and delivered for him what was seen as sub-standard work. Whatever the cause, the effect was a truly haunted, abandoned performance from Hedren and more grist to Connery's mill. Mark Rutland may move with the grace of Bond, he may even appear to be wearing the same hair piece

– Connery still not ready to reveal his receding hairline to the world – and he may speak with the obvious sophisticated knowledge of his nagging alter ego. Indeed, Rutland appears to be the erstwhile hero of the piece.

But beneath the surface, he is ultimately a predator, one who claims to 'hunt' his prey out of love, but in Connery's cold, calculated delivery that motive quickly, and rightly, becomes suspect. One of Bond's key elements was his cruelty, bordering on sadism at times; that cruelty runs rampant in Mark Rutland. It is only Connery's charm and on-screen charisma – elements that Hitchcock obviously recognized as vital – that hide the inherent misogyny of this man who sets out to melt the frigidity of his prey, his catch. It was a brave role for Connery to take on, one that cleverly afforded audiences a certain recognition factor, while subtly allowing him to broaden his range considerably.

The movie received divided notices, but many praised Connery, including *Films & Filming*, which wrote: 'Connery has real acting ability, and unless the James Bond things ruin him, I think he will provide audiences with enjoyable moments for many years to come.'

This was just the kind of comment the actor wanted to hear, the very reason in fact he'd agreed to Bond in the first place (that and the money, of course). But what was the point of good reviews if

Toupée be damned! – Connery on location in Spain, The Hill *(1965)* ☆

nobody went to see your film? *Marnie* was what is politely called a box-office disappointment and Sean Connery found himself saving Fort Knox, increasingly frustrated at being back playing at Bond in *Goldfinger*.

The actor had tried to move away from the persona, the image that most people perceived him as. In many ways, of course, it was a testament to his acting abilities that people so readily saw the man and the part as indistinguishable from each other, but it was the worry of where this left him in the long term – and his increasingly hostile relationship with Eon, largely financially based – that was more and more leading him away from the life of the shaken, not stirred Martini. It was potentially a huge move to make, but Connery knew two things: he was in this for the long run, and, having devoted himself to acting, he wanted to be as good at it as he could be. The idea of being typecast as Bond negated both of these.

Ironically, when a prime opportunity came for a role and a movie diametrically opposed to the Technicolor opulence of all things Bond, the actor at first turned it down.

The Hill was based on an original TV play by screenwriter Ray Rigby and R. S. Allen, and detailed the story of five new British military inmates, recently arrived at a desert stockade, ruled with a fist of iron by the army warders. The film was a stark, brutal examination of how the army strove to break down its own di............. attempt to rebuild them as regi.......... men. It presaged Kubrick's similarly themed *Full Metal Jacket* by more than two decades.

On location in Rome with Diane Cilento, who was filming *The Agony and the Ecstasy*, Connery mulled over Rigby's powerful script and opted to sign on for the role of Trooper Joe Roberts, the prisoner who decides to press charges against Drill Sergeant Williams (a brilliant performance from Ian Hendry), after his intense punishment of another prisoner by running him up and down the titular man-made hill, results in the inmate's death.

There were, as ever, conditions to be met. Despite the film's low-budget nature, Connery demanded $400,000, more than the rest of the cast put together and, at that time, commensurate with just about any major Hollywood star. The fee was agreed to and having Connery's name attached allowed producer Kenneth Hyman to not only raise the budget but attract the American director Sidney Lumet to the project.

Lumet, whose CV already boasted such groundbreaking movies as *Twelve Angry Men*, *Fail Safe* and *The Pawnbroker* (and would later add such seventies classics as *Dog Day Afternoon* to the list), brought a striking realism and power to the

LEFT *Diane Cilento with her two future Robin Hoods – Sean and son Jason Connery, 1965* ☆

RIGHT *In a rare post-Bond TV appearance, Connery joins Millicent Martin on* The Heart of Show Business *(1967)* ☆

movie. Filming in stark black and white under the punishing heat of the Spanish sun, in a specially constructed stockade set near Almeira, Lumet created a powerful impression of the claustrophobic reality of the five inmates' cramped cell, but also showed the breadth of the camp in all his exterior shots, constantly setting the action against a backdrop of hundreds of extras, relentlessly being put through their paces.

Connery was impressed with the director's approach, and would go on to make four more movies with him. 'He doesn't waste time or waffle,' he has said, 'and he knows what a picture costs and he gets his money up to the hilt. He works his end. I remember on *The Hill*, there was a scene which needed 350 soldiers, and he turns up on the day, and he actually counts all of the soldiers and of course there are some missing, so he says, "OK. We don't go until all the soldiers are here."'

It was a tough shoot, with Lumet's strong, visually realistic approach requiring the actors to run up the thirty-foot hill – carrying full army kit – for numerous takes. The portly comedy character actor Roy Kinnear was barely up to it and collapsed at one point, while just about everybody involved came down with dysentery – Connery included, who lost two days of filming.

From his superb British cast, Lumet elicited a number of outstanding performances – Hendry's

Connery, scotch in hand, regales comedian turned director Mike Nichols and Julie Andrews

cold-as-ice, borderline psychotic Williams, Harry Andrews's brilliantly brutal, justified 'by the book' RSM, Roy Kinnear's never-better snivelling scrounger and Ossie Davis's eccentric West Indian whisky-drinking recruit. Best of the bunch, however, was Connery, showing a depth and a passion he had never before displayed on the big screen. Bond director Terence Young said it best: 'It was Spencer Tracy stuff. Remarkably good acting.'

The Hill was a pivotal film for Sean Connery in many ways. Not only did it show how seamlessly he could blend into an ensemble when required, it also showed what a fine actor he had become, suffusing his whole performance with a brooding intensity that slowly, but surely, boils up under that Spanish sun. As a result, the two moments where he finally breaks down – on parade in front of Andrews's bullying superior, and at the movie's tragic climax – are devastatingly effective, strong, powerful, but full of emotion and tragedy. He even left the rug at home for the first time.

It was in short, the best performance he had ever given on screen at that time, and still remains one of the highlights of his career.

The Hill was the kind of movie Sean Connery had hoped James Bond would allow him to make. It was entered as the British contender at Cannes that year, and secured numerous nominations from the British Academy Awards. The critics were highly supportive, and with toupée off and moustache grown, were beginning to wake up to the fact that maybe there was more to this Connery fellah than just his way with a femme fatale and a mad world dominator. Connery had high hopes for the film.

Part of the power of Lumet's film undoubtedly stems from his decision to film it as naturalistically as possible – using available light and dialogue recorded whilst filming (as opposed to overdubbing later). Unfortunately, this was also the film's undoing internationally; in America, it played with subtitles, the at-times obscured soundtrack – full as it was of English slang and Scottish brogue – proving incomprehensible to the American ear. Consequently, it did zilch at the all-important US box office, so while Sean Connery, then arguably the biggest box-office star in the world, was doing his best work to date, no one was watching.

Acutely aware of all things fiscal from his audition for *South Pacific* to the present day, Connery knew that despite the undoubted quality of *The Hill*, he had still not made the break he needed to make from 007. Having the critics behind you was good, but Connery had a need to prove that audiences wanted to see him as an actor, not just as a secret agent.

Ultimately he rated the success of a movie by his own standards , what it had offered him and what he had achieved in his performance. And, as

he had shown with Broccoli and Saltzman at his first meeting, if this was not appreciated he was content to walk away and let the rest get on with it.

But still he knew how others rated success – at the box office. And he knew that America was important. Hollywood was still the film capital of the world, and acceptance there was crucial for him if there was to be life after Bond. If he was still in the game, and at this point he was *very* much in the game, he wanted to win.

So, for his next veer away from Bond, Connery headed back to America, to take on the role of a wayward, drunken poet penning a modern epic poem in contemporary Greenwich Village, in Irvin Kershner's *A Fine Madness*. It was a brash performance, in a very modish movie, one that was certainly entertaining, but seemed more like a sidestep after the intensity of his work in *The Hill*.

It was also another box-office failure.

These continued disappointments, coupled with the shock of encountering full-scale Bondmania on his subsequent trip to Japan for the filming of *You Only Live Twice*, finally convinced Sean Connery that, at least at this point in time, he would never be bigger than Bond. What he could be was separate, and damn the consequences.

He walked away from the biggest franchise in movie history – making way for an Australian

Back in the good old days, when Sean Connery was still talking to his Bond producer, Albert R. 'Cubby' Broccoli ☆

model named George Lazenby and, following on, his old friend Roger Moore.

As one Connery was doffing his tuxedo, another was donning one. In a desperate attempt to exploit the global success of 007, Italian producer Dorio Sabatello hired Sean's younger brother and full-time plasterer Neil Connery for a spoof movie entitled *Operation Kid Brother*, also released in some territories as the even less subtle *OK Connery*. Neil wore the tux, got the girls and the gadgets – he even had the cast, co-starring alongside *From Russia With Love* beauty Daniela Bianchi, *Thunderball* bad guy Adolfo Celi, and series regulars Bernard Lee and Lois Maxwell. In place of a gun, he had a bow and arrow, and for a world-beating villain, he had a man who made radioactive carpets! The movie was awash with bad gags and knowing references to big brother, and, all in all, was a cheap, exploitative shambles.

Big brother himself was none too pleased, telling Sabatello that 'by getting my brother to make this kind of picture, you are exploiting us both'. The producer responded by asking Sean to pose for a publicity photo with his sibling to show his backing of the project. He declined in no uncertain terms.

While his baby brother was wrestling with potentially lethal rugs, Connery was becoming actively involved in political issues in his native

homeland. Never a man to even so much as vote before, Connery now realized he was in a position to help what he saw as important or worthy causes. In March 1967, he publicly lent his support to the Scottish National Party.

Further evidence of the actor's politicization came with his decision to turn film director for the first and – so far – the only time in his career. The result was *The Bowler and the Bunnet*, a documentary look at an experimental collaboration between the trade unions, government and private enterprise that was keeping open a shipyard in Clyde, Scotland.

'With my background I know a bit about trade unions and all the problems,' he said, 'and what made me want to do the film in the first place was that Stewart [project director, Sir Iain Stewart] was doing something at Fairfields that hadn't been done so successfully anywhere in the country, England included. He was bridging that terrible gulf between the bosses and the workers and he was breaking down the petty suspicions between unions. It was all going famously and production was going up. It was something to shout about.'

Connery later explained the depth of feeling he had for this most personal of projects. 'What that documentary did for me in personal terms was to make me realize that part of me belonged to that kind of background. I thought I'd left it all behind me. I thought I'd been liberated from that claustrophobic, John Knoxian narrow environment. Well, I had in a way, because of the lifestyle connected with the Bond films, but I knew I just couldn't turn my back on it completely.'

Television companies had no such problem, however. The film aired on local Scottish television, but, perhaps because of its overt political nature, Connery was unable to get either the BBC or ITV to give it a national airing.

By now it was nearly a year since Connery had been on a film set. As well as making his documentary and exploring the political landscape of his homeland, he found time to design the cover for his wife's first novel, a showbusiness satire called *The Manipulators*. For his abstract-art cover design, Connery was paid £30. Not the kind of money he was used to making. It was time for him to get back on the big screen, to see what his career held for him at this pivotal moment. He decided to do so in the guise of the world's first Scottish cowboy.

4. The Character

Sean Connery persuaded Eon to release him from his contract for his final Bond film, by agreeing to a pay day of £50,000 plus overtime and a percentage of the profits on what should have been his penultimate appearance. The shoot on *You Only Live Twice* was so protracted, however, that the actor picked up an additional £170,000 in overages. The most important thing, though, was that he was now a free agent, and one who opted to set his price for future work at $200,000 plus 5 per cent of the box office, or a flat $400,000 if he forsook his percentage.

Before deciding on his next big-screen foray, however, Connery decided to turn theatrical impresario. He had given it a shot the year before while filming *A Fine Madness* in New York, when he attempted to mount a Broadway production of Ted Allan Herman's play, *The Secret of the World*. Shelley Winters was due to star, with Connery on board as first-time director. The project, however, never materialized.

But in early 1967, he succeeded in transferring an Oxford Playhouse production of Ben Jonson's *Volpone*, with Leo McKern and Leonard Rossiter, to the

Drumming up business
for Scotland's first
cowboy hero, Connery
with Shalako co-star
Brigitte Bardot, 1968 ☆

Robert Shaw got him started, and golf soon became one of the great loves of Connery's life ☆

Garrick Theatre in London's West End, where it enjoyed a successful run.

Producer Euan Lloyd was the first to bite at Connery's new movie price tag, offering the Scot a surprising role – the lead in a British-backed western, based on Louis L'Amour's novel *Shalako*. Ever since his first trips to the local cinema in Fountainbridge, westerns had been a favourite of Connery's. The money was right, the notion of playing a cowboy was right, and the unique nature of the film was right.

The cast looked pretty good too – Brigitte Bardot was top-lining alongside Connery, while Pussy Galore herself, Honor Blackman, was reuniting with the former 007 on screen for the first time. Playing the somewhat atypical role of an English butler in the wild west was British comedian – and Connery's golfing buddy – Eric Sykes.

Shortly before filming began, Connery was ticketed for speeding, a minor incident which would have gone unnoticed had it not been for the fact that the police officer who stopped him was named James Bond. 'Ever since the case arose I've been pestered out of my life by film and publicity men,' said Sergeant James Bond at the time.

It was also around this time that Joe Connery retired and finally allowed his wealthy movie-star son to move him and Effie out of Fountainbridge.

As he headed Spain-wards to shoot *Shalako*, Connery explained his current situation and no-nonsense attitude to the press. 'I suppose the real difference between me and me a few years ago is that I've reached the age where I realize that one day I'm going to die. I talked to Tony Quinn about it and he said, "Once you've realized this, the next thing is to get your priorities straight." And that's what I'm trying to do. I'm almost thirty-seven and I realize I'm more than halfway there. So I intend to get the most out of life doing creative things with a few talented people around me. I won't put up with bores any longer, or have people living off my back.'

Connery involved himself with all aspects of the *Shalako* project right from the off, joining producer Lloyd in location scouting, first in Mexico, and then in Spain, once again near Almeira, where the movie was eventually shot. (The area had been used to great effect in Sergio Leone's recent trilogy of '*Dollars*' movies.) Connery arrived on set two weeks early to practise horse riding, and by the time his co-stars joined him, he was as Eric Sykes recalled 'a very proficient horseman'.

As he had always tried to do, and would insist on being able to do from now on, Connery also involved himself heavily in the script. 'We were sitting side by side in the sunshine in Spain learning our lines,' Sykes later recalled. 'I noticed that every so often he would tear half a page, or even a whole page, of dialogue out of his script and throw it on the floor. There was a pile of a dozen or more screwed-up pieces of paper, so I asked him why he was tearing these bits out. He said it was unnecessary crap that was not needed. He was actually editing his part as he went along, apparently without reference to the director, Eddie Dmytryk.'

During production, tempers flared and at one point Bardot threatened to quit. It was left to Connery to smooth the waters. In fact – along with his unofficial role as script editor – the actor bore a great deal of the weight of *Shalako*'s production, and as filming progressed he quickly became aware that the movie was not working; even before shooting had finished, he knew that this would, like his other recent non-spy movies, not be the one to lay the ghost of Bond to rest.

Addressing the press at the time of the film's release, Connery made it only too clear how aware he was of the power of the Bond image, hinting that taking on such an iconic figure as the cowboy was his attempt to provide another equally strong archetype, laying into reviewers who dismissed his performance as one-dimensional. 'For this film, a cardboard character is all you want,' he explained. 'They were going to try and give him a lot of depth and background, but in a western like this, we decided to keep him a mystery figure. The public seem to like an image. I've broken away from the Bond one and given them another, I hope.' Image was clearly an important subject for Connery at the time.

"Sometimes I think if I'd been smart, I'd have hired a publicity office to keep a parallel image going for me the whole time during the Bond thing,' he openly speculated in the press. "It might have made it easier for me. They were such a phenomenal success, you see, that anything else I tried to do counted for nothing. But I kept thinking: just to create another image for myself, is it worth it? After all, they'd just be two sides of the same Mickey Mouse coin and neither would be me anyway.'

When Connery wasn't in front of the camera, he could by now often be found on the fairways of the world. After Robert Shaw had introduced him to the game of golf, Connery had seriously studied it prior to his on-screen match with Auric Goldfinger. Now it was a passion, almost unequalled in his life. He played in numerous tournaments around the world, and would later run his own to raise money for the Scottish charity he was shortly to found. 'To me it's a complete revelation of all of my shortcomings and problems,' he once said of the game: 'Temper, ego, feeling, thinking. That's why it's so therapeutic. It almost gives you a philosophy, which is a great help to somebody like myself who doesn't have a religion.'

Connery poses on the

golf course ☆

*Leaving Bond behind and
going down the pit,
Connery on location for* The
Molly Maguires, *1968* ☆

Sean Connery was heading towards his fortieth year. And while it was true that the likes of Cary Grant could happily go on romancing women half their age on screen (something Connery himself would do in the later stages of his career), Connery was more than aware of the potential limitations of the ageing leading man. Ever the pragmatist, he once again sought to reinvent himself, this time as a character actor. He would still take leading man roles obviously, but within them he would subtly shift his audience's perception of him. Tellingly, he never sought to achieve this by playing villainous

parts, he knew there was something innately heroic about Sean Connery on screen, regal even – he would later play Kings Arthur and Richard, as well as Agamemnon and an immortal.

He began by remodelling the image – Sean Connery over the next few years was rarely seen under a toupée or without his increasingly droopy moustache, with this altered appearance acting as a form of visual punctuation to further separate the man from James Bond. It would for the most part – barring a short-lived return to the Bond fold – be the most experimental period of Connery's career,

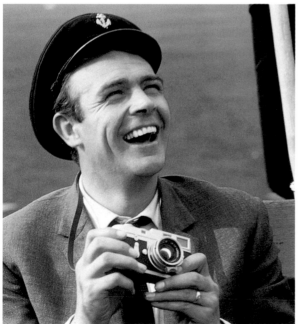

TOP *Early publicity shot for Connery as Bond* ☆

ABOVE *Snap-happy during filming of* From Russia With Love ☆

RIGHT *Relaxing on deck* ☆

82 ☆ SEAN CONNERY

Connery sneaks off for a rendezvous with his other great love ☆

ABOVE *With co-star Ursula Andress,* Dr No *(1962)* ☆

TOP RIGHT *A subtly shifting image, with Tippi Hedren in Hitchcock's* Marnie *(1964)* ☆

RIGHT *Poster art for* Shalako *(1968)* ☆

A crown, but not so much as an Oscar nomination, The Man Who Would Be King *(1975)* ☆

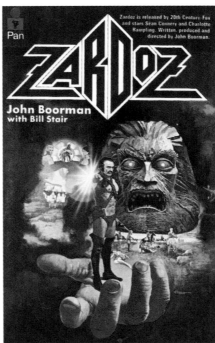

FAR LEFT *Out of red nappy, with Zardoz co-star Charlotte Rampling* ☆

LEFT *Maybe somewhere, in this 1974 novelization, Zardoz actually makes sense (or maybe not...)* ☆

Five Days One
Summer *(1983)* ☆

LEFT *Out on the town with (from left to right) wife Micheline, son Jason and stepson Paul* ☆

BELOW *The law wears Armani, The Untouchables (1987)* ☆

ABOVE *The world's most viable OAP action hero,* The Rock *(1996)* ☆

RIGHT *Inter-generational icons –*
Indiana Jones, plus 'Dad' ☆

Big smiles! – With Catherine Zeta Jones, publicizing Entrapment *(1999)* ☆

during which he would produce some of his finest work (*The Man Who Would Be King, The Wind and the Lion*), and some of his weakest and weirdest (*Zardoz* is coming – be warned!). At times he would work in the kind of role and with the kind of people he had always aspired to; at other times, he would appear to be woefully misguided, floundering and inadvertently destroying a career that had once belonged to the most popular movie star on the planet. For more than a decade, Sean Connery would search and seek to find where he now belonged on the big screen.

It was most undoubtedly Connery's involvement with the shipyards of Fairfields and his making of *The Bowler and the Bunnet* that drew him to his next movie, *The Molly Maguires*.

Budgeted at a considerable $11 million, the movie told the tale of the unionization of a group of Irish immigrants in the Pennsylvania coal mines of the 1870s. Richard Harris was set to co-star, and the four-month shoot began in April of 1968. Connery had first discussed the project with director Martin Ritt back in 1966, when he was visiting Diane Cilento on the set of Ritt's Paul Newman-starring western *Hombre*. True to his word, when Ritt raised the finance to make the film, Connery was there, once again intrigued by the quality of the material and once again hoping that

would translate into audiences at the box office. It didn't; and neither did his next venture, the Russian-Italian co-production, *The Red Tent*. Connery filmed for three weeks in Moscow. 'I was very aware of the fear element,' he once recalled. 'Every day they changed my driver, so I would never know who my driver was. We'd drive to Mosfilm – it was bigger than all the American film studios put together – and they made you go through this ritual every day of checking who you were, like it was a Swiss bank or something. And the interpreters were all invariably KGB. You had no knowledge of how anything worked. There was no sense of time or programme. No urgency about anything in filming the production. Took for ever to light and shoot. In fact, they just had a whole different concept of time, and it was reflected in the movie, which ran four hours something in Russia and two hours in America when Paramount bought it. And everybody seemed to have something to say about how the film should be made, in the worst kind of way, and yet it got made, and it was a huge success because it was the first time Russia had made a picture with any other country. A big internal success. Never a success anywhere else.'

It rapidly disappeared from sight on release, but proving Connery's still potent star power, he usurped Peter Finch's top billing, who spent nine months on the movie; Connery spent three weeks.

*Directing wife Diane Cilento
and new house-guest Robert
Hardy in Ted Allan
Herman's stage play,* I've
Seen You Cut Lemons, *in
December 1969. It closed
the same month* ☆

Following his journey to Moscow, the actor made a brief – his last to date – return to television. In February 1969, he appeared in one of a trio of plays by Alun Owen. Taking the lead in the first of these, *MacNeil*, Connery appeared on the cover of that week's *TV Times*, his interview inside stressing how he was using this television appearance to fight against the enduring image of Bond.

But the Bond movies were going strong as ever. Repackaged as double bills and re-released to American cinemas, they were still proving to be huge money earners. Even the latest film, *On Her Majesty's Secret Service*, with George Lazenby now in place, had proved a sizeable global hit. But the producers, and in many ways the audience, were not happy with Lazenby. What they all really wanted was to have Connery back, at least one more time. Advances were made, with co-producer Stanley Sopel opening a discourse with the actor - it was clear by then he wouldn't deal with either Broccoli or Saltzman – but Connery was still saying never again.

On screen, Connery's new ventures were failing to find an audience and everyone still wanted him – and more importantly, still thought of him – as James Bond. Off screen, meanwhile, Connery's world was changing significantly. His marriage to Diane Cilento was rapidly coming to an end, this time irretrievably, something that was exacerbated when he met a woman named Micheline Roquebrune at a golf tournament in Marrakesh. She was married at the time, but later said of their first meeting, 'I think I was in love with him from the first look.'

In 1970, spurred on by his work on *The Bowler and the Bunnet*, and his growing friendship with Sir Iain Stewart, Connery founded the Scottish International Education Trust. It was a charity designed to call on Scottish émigrés from all over the world, to lend support to the young and underprivileged of their home country, in an attempt to build up the industry, arts and education of the country from within. 'Scots abroad owe their country something,' he said at the time, 'and I'm after at least £1 a head from émigrés. There's obviously something wrong if Scots keep abandoning their country. What we are trying to do is improve the country so that people will not be so ready to move.'

He set the ball rolling himself with an initial donation of £17,000 which he had raised from organizing a recent pro-am golf tournament. During the following decade, when Connery was seen as often on television in such pro-am events as

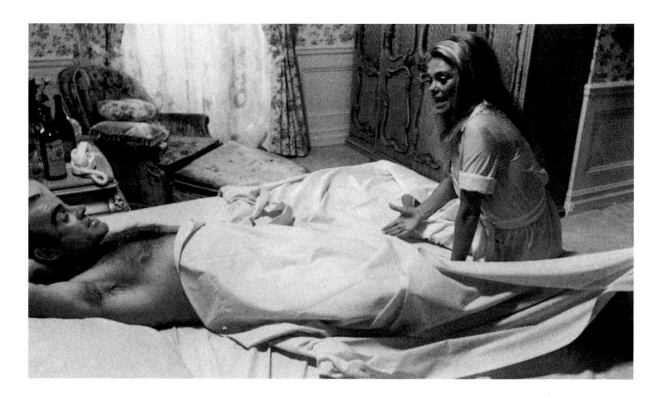

Looking to make a killing, Connery with Dyan Cannon in Sidney Lumet's The Anderson Tapes *(1971)* ☆

he was on a movie screen, his motivation – apart from the game, of course – was to continue funding his trust (the money was administered through Dunbar and Co., the private bank of which he had become a director).

Away from such charitable works, Connery was busy writing a screenplay for *Macbeth*; he spent many months on the project and had planned to possibly direct and star, but abandoned it when he learned that Roman Polanski was at work on a similarly modern interpretation of the play.

It was Diane Cilento who suggested Connery direct her and Robert Hardy in Ted Allan Herman's play *I've Seen You Cut Lemons*. Connery leapt into the task, persuading Hardy to move in with the couple so that, having rehearsed all day, the three of them could spend their evenings discussing the play. Hardy was apparently bemused by what the Connerys called a 'think tank' which occupied an

upstairs room, and in which they would both spend time of a morning focusing their energies.

The play opened in Oxford in 1969 and briefly toured the country before reaching the West End, where it promptly closed after five days. Then it was back to the movies for Connery.

Sidney Lumet's next project was a prescient combination of surveillance paranoia and elaborate heist movie. Connery signed on for the lead as the head of a motley crew who aim to rob an entire Manhattan apartment block and, in *The Anderson Tapes*, found what he'd been looking for, a decent hit at the American box office.

In February 1971, unable or unwilling to juggle their conflicting careers and increasingly limited home life, Sean Connery and Diane Cilento separated. She moved out, he sold the family home, and was soon spending more and more time with Micheline Roquebrune.

Some felt Connery was just walking through his return as James Bond; here he is clearly sleeping through it, during Diamonds Are Forever *(1971)* ☆

In the meantime, the Bond people were trying to get him back into the tux. It was David Picker, head of United Artists in the US, who finally twisted the arm of the hard-dealing Scot. He flew to London, met with Connery and thrashed out a deal at the Dorchester hotel, a deal which landed Connery in excess of $1 million, plus a percentage.

There were numerous reasons why Connery chose to step back into the role he had tried so hard to escape. Money was clearly one of them – although the actor passed on his million dollars to the Scottish International Education Trust. Ego obviously played a part. The films he'd made since Bond hadn't set the world on fire, and there was inevitably a large amount of satisfaction in that, having tried George Lazenby, the producers clearly thought they were a lot better off with Sean. The role might have made him, but this proved that he had made the role.

He might be stuck with being associated with James Bond, but at least he was being seen as the one and only James Bond. Despite what Broccoli had said, the actor was at least as big as the role, no longer subsumed by it.

It was late in the day when Connery signed on to make *Diamonds Are Forever*. So late, in fact, that an American actor, John Gavin, had been signed as the new Bond. He was promptly paid off and Connery slipped back into his old role with his customary ease and grace, although he did try to get the hairpieces thinned out.

'Age is as inevitable as tomorrow,' he argued. 'Nobody is immortal, not me, not you and not James Bond. The fascination for looking young is the joke of all time.'

Unlike his last experience as 007, *Diamonds Are Forever* proved to be a well-organized, efficient shoot that wrapped on time, thus not allowing Connery to invoke the overtime clause in his lengthy contract.

Diamonds Are Forever was a curiously unbalanced Bond movie, though, with elements of Fleming's original novel uncomfortably grafted on to a loose plot revolving around the arch-villain Blofeld, here played by Charles Gray. (Gray had also appeared in *You Only Live Twice*, though not as Blofeld.) Connery was keen to play Bond as an older man, and while he didn't manage to persuade the producers to drop the hairpiece, he made sure there was enough grey in it to show that the lean, lithe hero of *Dr No* was now hitting middle age.

The character was also subtly altered here, moving further and further away from Connery's original interpretation of Ian Fleming's hero, heading more towards the jokier version of Bond that Roger Moore would assume with ease and an arched eyebrow. It was also clear that the Bond franchise was coming to rely more and more heavily on gimmicks and gadgets – the Moon Buggy sequence comes out of nowhere and remains unexplained, save for the toy spin-off possibilities, and at one point Blofeld appears in drag. Not a good image for any super-villain, let alone the head of SPECTRE.

Nonetheless, financially at least, the film did the job, proving once again that Bond – especially Connery as Bond – was unbeatable, grossing nearly $100 million around the world, making it the biggest film of the year.

Still, Connery was adamant that this was his last time out as 007 and his arrival at the UK premiere of the film with friend Roger Moore acted as a public passing of the torch, since Moore would take over the role in 1973's *Live and Let Die*.

This was a period of considerable upheaval in Connery's life, what with one failed marriage, a temporary return to Her Majesty's Secret Service and the ongoing need to establish himself as a presence in movies without a licence to kill. The period became even more marked when Connery's father Joe died in March 1972. 'He was sixty-nine, my father, and somehow I had never thought of him

*Out on his own, Connery
tackles one of his
strongest roles, in 1972's*
The Offence ☆

dying. He was such a contented man. And when he
did die it was a great stopper for me. It brought me
up with a tremendous jolt,' he said. 'I had retired
him when he was about sixty and he was loving
every minute of it. Now he's dead and it's a sobering
experience, more than I ever realized it would be.
You know, there's a saying in the Masai tribe that
you are not a man until your father dies. If that is
true, then it's a pretty stiff price to pay.'

As part of the deal he had thrashed out with Picker,
Connery had persuaded United Artists to back two
movies of his choice – each budgeted at less than $1
million. For the first of these, he opted to adapt
John Hopkins's play, *This Story of Yours*, a tense
psychological drama that follows the police
interrogation of a suspected paedophile. Retitled
The Offence, Connery was to play the detective

whose intense brutalization of his suspect results in
the prisoner's death within custody. He surrounded
himself with a number of familiar faces – Ian
Bannen from *The Hill*, Vivien Merchant, whom he
had appeared opposite on stage in *Judith*, and old
friend Trevor Howard. In the director's chair,
Connery as head of his own company, Tantallon
Films, placed Sidney Lumet.

The movie was a tough, uncompromising affair,
and featured one of Connery's best ever
performances, certainly his best since *The Hill*.

'I played a policeman who brings in a child
molester and beats him to death. As a result, the
policeman discovers that he harboured more malice
in his head than the monster he was after and slowly
begins to come apart. In a sense, the cop could be
called bad, but the movie showed that evil happens
for both the best and the worst of reasons. Such

'I was clad in nothing but thigh-high red boots, bandoliers and a red nappy.': Zardoz (1973) ☆

complexity appeals to me as an actor and as an individual.' It was, however, a difficult subject handled in a relentlessly bleak way and, despite its limited budget, had trouble scaring up anything approaching an audience when it was released later that year. 'It cost something like £920,000 and I think it took ten years to break even. Still, it was worth it, because it was a good picture to make.'

Although Connery contracted John Hopkins to work on a screenplay based on the life of the explorer Sir Richard Burton, and commissioned feminist writer Germaine Greer to pen a treatment for a movie based around an Aboriginal culture, Tantallon's second film with UA never materialized after the failure of its first.

Connery's career after Bond was not working out. Despite a diversity of roles, and some fine performances, Sean Connery as an actor was rapidly losing his bankability. Just as he sought to show an image of a man approaching middle life, a realistic man more than a cartoonish secret agent, he was finding that the world didn't really want to know. Of course, on the surface he appeared to be unperturbed by such things, insisting that the work spoke for itself, but after the failure of *The Offence*, coupled with the death of his father and his ongoing divorce negotiations, Connery decided to retreat from the big screen to regroup and reassess. He headed for the fairways of Spain, Micheline Roquebrune his now constant companion.

Rather than plan his next cinematic venture to address the issues that obviously concerned him, Connery decided to act spontaneously, signing on for a new science-fiction film by John Boorman, as a last-minute replacement for an injured Burt Reynolds. The movie was *Zardoz*, and if Connery hoped that it would restore shine to his star, he was in for a big disappointment.

'I was absolutely caught by its originality,' Connery said of Boorman's script, 'and I read it through twice and telephoned John the following morning. It was one of the best ideas I'd come across for ages, and I'd been reading about two scripts a day. What gripped me especially was the direction the people in it were taking in this future existence, as opposed to spaceships and rockets and all that.'

Somewhere, in someone's mind – possibly even John Boorman's – *Zardoz* makes sense. To the rest of us, it hasn't a chance. Full of flying heads, 'the gun is good, the penis is bad'-style dialogue, a camp John Alderton and a frankly indecipherable plot, *Zardoz* is quite simply the daftest film Sean Connery has ever been associated with.

'The Renegades abhor the system and fight it,' he once said, desperately trying to make sense of the film's confused story line, 'and put on records of Peggy Lee songs and perpetuate the old ballroom dancing and hang on to the old rituals because they are not in accord with the way things are. On the other hand, the Apathetics are reluctant to do anything.' Mmm . . . ballroom-dancing renegades – sounds like a winner!

Set in the year 2293, (which looks remarkably like a farmhouse in 1970s Ireland), Connery – wearing his knickers and six guns – is cast as the most virile man on Earth (typecasting!), in a movie that is awash with reams of bungled philosophizing on the nature of man.

On the admittedly limited plus side, *Zardoz* does boast a wonderfully bad scene in which the leaders of the future try to give Connery an erection, and comes complete with one of the most inadvertently

hilarious endings in cinema history. Nonetheless, Connery retained fond memories of it. 'I was covered in mud which was actually cement dust and earth. It was agony, because when it hardened it stuck to my chest hair and tore it all out. Added to which I was clad in nothing but thigh-high red boots, bandoliers and a red nappy. And we had so little money that the extras in the background were Irish guys with red-painted legs instead of boots and their Y-fronts dyed red.'

During filming, Boorman once asked his leading man why he never lost his Scottish accent, no matter what the part called for. 'Because I wouldn't know who the fuck I was,' came the curt reply.

Connery made himself a guest in the Boorman household during the duration of filming, ensuring that he paid Boorman's wife his 'rent' every week. He also renegotiated the discount deal for the rest of the cast at a local hotel, getting a lower price than Boorman had managed and, when adding up the cost of his car and driver, went to Boorman with another offer: 'I'll tell you what I'll do. I'll drive myself and split it with you.'

Both *Zardoz* and the next film, the dull hijack drama *Ransom*, were resounding commercial and critical disasters, but Connery's next movie would go some way to repairing that. Teaming once again with director Sidney Lumet, Connery joined the all-star cast of *Murder on the Orient Express*. While the

All aboard! Connery and Vanessa Redgrave, awaiting their train, in Murder on the Orient Express *(1974)* ☆

film was hugely popular, Connery's role as the stuffy Colonel Arbuthnot was simply one of many star turns in the film. People weren't going to the movies just to see Sean Connery. However, what was more important about the actor's role in this Agatha Christie extravaganza was how it paved the way for his next three movies. Finding himself at home in period costume, Connery would remain there – albeit in three different periods – for a trio of movies that would see the actor delivering some of his best work and, slowly, finding his place back on the big screen.

In October 1973, Sean Connery's divorce from Diane Cilento was finalized. Having always done his best to keep his private life away from the prying eyes of the press, Connery reasserted his intentions to the reporters gathered outside the courtroom. 'As from this day I will have no comment to make on my private life. Nothing of my private life will ever be divulged to the press with whom I do not have an especially good relationship, because I have no press agent. To simplify matters, I intend now to keep private matters private.'

The following year was a time of immense change for Sean Connery – including a change of address. When the new Labour government came to power that year, Connery decided to make Marbella his permanent residence. The move was

Spot the Arab! Connery and friend, in 1975's The Wind and the Lion ☆

for tax reasons, after Labour raised the level of income tax to eighty-three per cent for those in the movie-star bracket. As much as he loved his home in Spain, the warm winters and the availability of a decent golf course at the bottom of the garden, years later Connery was still bitter about the move.

'When I left in 1974 you could get a pound for a dollar and Denis Healey, this wonderful Chancellor who bankrupted the country, said he was going to squeeze the rich pips till they squeaked, or some bloody thing, sitting with his apartment in town and his farm and his house up in Hampstead, living like a gangster on all this socialist whatever, and their answer was to put the taxes up. Well I was paying ninety-eight per cent tax. I was one of the most successful actors around and I didn't have a pot to piss in.'

At the time Connery severed nearly all his ties with Britain, selling his properties and businesses; his one remaining tie was his affiliation with the Scottish International Education Trust.

The man who had once been the most popular actor in the world was now divorced and middle-aged. His box-office drawing power severely diminished, he was rapidly being outpaced by a whole new generation of leading men, talents such as Jack Nicholson, Al Pacino, Dustin Hoffman. In the hands of Roger Moore, Bond was becoming a parody of his former self, while Connery was becoming ever more anachronistic, still carrying the baggage that comes with being a sixties icon. To move forward, he decided to head backwards.

He also decided to head for Hollywood. Or, more importantly, have Hollywood come to him. After all, his self-imposed exile meant that he was only allowed to spend ninety days a year in Britain, effectively ending his working relationship with his home country for many years after.

There has always been something larger than life about Sean Connery. There's a certain nobility, a certain imperiousness, a confident arrogance that sees him easily fit the shoes of great men, of leaders. For his next three pivotal movies, Connery brought these attributes to bear in a trio of period adventure movies that re-established him as an actor, and as a man embracing middle age rather than denying it, whether as a nomadic Arab in *The Wind and the Lion*, a British soldier with delusions of omnipotence in *The Man Who Would Be King*, or as an ageing Robin Hood, forever tied to his legend while slowly confronting his own mortality.

John Milius is an iconoclastic film-maker and the author of such myth-breaking movies as *The Life and Times of Judge Roy Bean* and *Apocalypse Now*. As such he didn't seem to mind that the man he wanted to play the lead character in his new movie – a turn-of-the-century Berber named El Raisuli – spoke with a Scottish accent. 'Connery is a terrific actor and looks very much like an Arab,' the writer-director argued. 'In fact, he looks not unlike the Ayatollah.'

Milius's film was loosely based on a true story from the early 1900s, and saw Candice Bergen cast as a young American woman in North Africa, kidnapped by the Berber tribe led by Connery's Raisuli. Raisuli in no way harms the woman – in fact tellingly in the film, they never touch – and out of this situation develops a curious kind of romance.

'I adored the writing immediately,' said Connery of the film. 'The kidnapping of hostages, the Islamic code, and the American intervention had terrific scope.'

Strange as it may seem, Sean Connery had never played a romantic lead before *The Wind and the Lion*. Sexy, yes, he'd done that, but romance was something new for him on screen, and at that time it was unusual to see a balding, grey-streaked man playing just such a role. It was a hugely influential shift in his career, not only leading to talk of the middle-aged sex symbol, but offering Connery a wide variety of roles over the subsequent years, for which, more often than not, any other actor his age would be out of the running.

If *The Wind and the Lion* showed a new romantic charisma in its leading man, then his next film simply showed the world what a remarkably fine actor he had grown into. John Huston had been working on his adaptation of Rudyard Kipling's *The Man Who Would Be King*, since the fifties, with everyone from Humphrey Bogart and Clark Gable to Peter O'Toole and Richard Burton attached to play the two leads. By 1973, Huston was in talks with Paul Newman to play one of those roles, when Newman offered up the following advice: 'I think this is one of the best plays I've ever read. But honestly, I don't think it is for me. I reckon the two roles should be played by Englishmen. For Chrissakes, John, get Connery and Caine.'

Huston did just that with both actors delighted finally to have the opportunity to work together. It took two years of waiting, but come 1975 everything was in place and production began.

Shortly beforehand, Connery, ever evasive of the press, had flown to Gibraltar and married Micheline in the same registry office as his first marriage. He managed to keep the fact hidden for several months, the news only breaking during the filming of Huston's movie.

Connery and Caine, playing two working-class ex-British soldiers, spent hours rehearsing their repartee for the early part 'It was like watching a polished vaudeville act,' Huston recollected. 'Everything on cue – all I had to do was decide how best to shoot it.'

'While I'm inclined to wing it,' Caine once offered, 'I've always had the feeling that Sean has known his lines for weeks. He comes to the shoot so well rehearsed, it's as if he's spent hours in his bedroom going through all his moves.'

As indeed he does. Connery often spends time rehearsing his lines by playing all the parts and

doing all the voices in the privacy of his own room. 'Sean's a gifted mimic,' said Michael Crichton, a later director. 'He did startlingly accurate imitations of everyone in the cast of *The First Great Train Robbery*, including Donald [Sutherland] and Lesley-Anne [Down], his leading lady.'

The movie was shot largely in Morocco, and while on location in the remote town of Ouarzazate, Connery and Caine found themselves in a Muslim men-only, alcohol-free disco, where all the men danced with each other out of necessity. After a few Cokes, Connery asked Caine if he minded if he asked Caine's driver to dance (his own driver was deemed too ugly for a quick whirl around the dance floor). Caine had no objection and his driver willingly obliged the Scot, who contentedly bopped the night away.

The two actors had known each other since Connery's *South Pacific* days and had, over the years, become firm friends. This was their first opportunity to work together in a movie, and their natural chemistry contributes in large part in the success of Huston's film. Playing a happy-go-lucky opportunist who heads to the far-off land of Kafiristan to set himself up as its king, only to find himself consumed by the power he experiences once he has been mistaken for a god, not only offered Connery a wide range for his performance, but saw him building on the noble and imperious elements

Connery lords it over Michael Caine and Saeed Jaffrey in John Huston's pivotal The Man Who Would Be King *(1975)* ☆

he had brought to *The Wind and the Lion*. As John Huston once remarked of his performance: 'Sean is simply wonderful, especially when he thinks he's Alexander the Great,' (a role he had, of course, played back on television in 1961).

One scene in the movie also required him to stand in the middle of an extremely fragile-looking rope bridge, suspended over a 200-foot gorge. Connery inspected the site the day before the scene was to be shot and, with the wind blowing, only ventured a few feet out on to the structure. The next morning when he arrived on set, he voiced some trepidation. 'I was here yesterday and the bridge looked OK. But today it seems to be leaning over to the right,' he said.

'The bridge is exactly as it was yesterday, Sean,' Huston replied. 'The difference today is that you have to walk out on it, so you're looking at it from a different point of view.' The challenge was implicit – Connery responded by striding out to the middle of the bridge and nailing the shot.

Exhausted from his two desert adventures, Connery was all set to take some time off when a script arrived entitled *The Death of Robin Hood*. Here was a perfect opportunity – to portray a noted hero, but to show him as a mortal man, an ageing man realizing that his time has come. The title was changed to *Robin and Marian*, to emphasize the romantic aspects of the movie, with Audrey Hepburn returning to the screen after an eight-year absence to play Marian. 'They should have stuck with the title,' Connery said, 'because that is what it was about, and people were disappointed because from the new title they expected some stirring adventure. The whole thing was very much anti-mythic. This guy comes galloping back after eighteen years away on the crusades and says, "Hi, I'm back!" and of course no one cares much any more. And he's getting up each morning in the forest, and creaking and groaning and coughing and taking a leak in the bushes and it's all too much for a man of his age. They hated that idea in the States. They can't take the idea that a hero might be over the hill and falling apart.'

Having spent so many years trapped in a myth of his own making, Connery relished the opportunity to play such a myth-breaking part. The revisionist nature of Richard Lester's film failed to find an audience, but was a critical success, especially for Connery, who with his last three movies, had finally emerged from the shadow of James Bond only to head straight back to 007.

Kevin McClory had sold his rights to *Thunderball* for a ten-year period, but now that time was up and McClory was contemplating a remake, a new Bond film to rival the ongoing success of the official series. The movie was to be called 'James Bond of the Secret Service' (later renamed 'Warhead') and McClory, eager to involve Connery and knowing that no one knew the character as well as him, invited the actor to write the script with British spy novelist Len Deighton, creator of the Harry Palmer books and movie series, which had made a star out of Michael Caine.

Connery set to work on the script, for once planning on taking credit for a job he invariably performed on all his movies, but McClory faced stiff opposition from Eon and the project was delayed for some years due to various legal battles between both parties.

Having effectively reshaped his on-screen persona once again, and reaffirmed his star value for all the world to see, Connery instantly risked blowing it all with his next film. Indeed, for the next five years, Connery found himself rapidly moving backwards through a series of misjudged, or misfired movies, beginning with 1976's *The Next Man*, a lamentably dull political thriller that failed even to find a distributor in England, something that had never happened to a Sean Connery movie before. 'Basically, it was a good idea that went off half-cocked because we didn't have a good script,' Connery recalls. 'We tried to salvage it through editing, but that can never be done.'

The following year's *A Bridge Too Far*, Richard Attenborough's all-star recreation of the Allied

Deconstructing the mythology of an iconic hero, Robin and Marian *(1976)* ☆

defeat at Arnhem in 1944, was a worthier effort, and a high-profile movie, but, given the nature of such big-name ensembles, it was in no way dependent on Connery, or allowed him much room to command the film. Still, he was very useful, albeit unknowingly, in securing its cast. 'I will remember always that his presence in it made a tremendous difference to the quality and standard of actors who, once he had agreed, also then agreed to the movie,' said Attenborough. One of those who also signed up for duty was Michael Caine, who reportedly landed a role after a casual meeting with Attenborough and Connery, at which he politely pointed out that 'Everybody else is in this fucking film except me.'

Connery came on board for $350,000, believing that everyone was being paid in the same range, and was subsequently outraged when he learned

that Robert Redford was pocketing $2 million for his part. Connery was quickly on the phone to producer Joe Levine, who agreed to double the aggrieved actor's fee, blaming his agent for not securing him a better deal in the first place.

It wasn't Connery's agent, however, who was troubling him; it was his business manager Kenneth Richards. Richards had worked for Connery, managing his financial and business affairs since 1972. In early 1977, Connery's wife Micheline had become concerned over Richards's activities when she tried to locate a washing machine that had been removed from Connery's former London home. 'I asked Mr Richards what had happened,' explained Mrs Connery, 'and he told me he had given it to his son as a wedding present because it wouldn't work in Spain as the power supply was different. It made me wonder and I went on to investigate. It was the worst moment of my life when I discovered my suspicions were correct.' Her further investigations led her to discover that Richards had invested $3.25 million of Connery's money in a French property company that was now facing financial ruin. Richards was dismissed and Connery began what would become many years of litigation, between himself and his former trusted employee.

Back in uniform, from The Longest Day *to* A Bridge Too Far *(1977)* ☆

Maybe it was the sudden realization that he was not as well off as he imagined that kept Connery working at a flat-out pace for the rest of the decade; it certainly wasn't the quality of scripts landing on his mat.

The First Great Train Robbery was an amusing, though not terribly ambitious nineteenth-century caper movie, with the actor cast as Edward Pierce, a gentleman thief who schemes to rob a gold-bullion train. It was directed by Michael Crichton, who adapted the screenplay from his own novel. Connery initially rejected it, twice. 'It was pretty awful. It was very heavy and obvious. One was aware of the fact that it was a period piece in the worst sense.' Connery worked with Crichton on the rewrites and Crichton returned the favour by opting to film in Ireland, where Connery wouldn't be subject to British tax laws, instead of London, as originally planned.

Connery embraced the opportunity, as he so often did, to perform the majority of his own stunts in the movie, which in this case involved the film's climactic chase in which he ran along the top of a speeding steam train. 'Within minutes Connery was grinning like a kid on a carnival ride,' recalled Crichton, who also said that as his star quickly got horizontal to go under a bridge, he was heard to exclaim, 'Bloody fantastic!' The film was pleasant, with strong chemistry between Connery and his co-star Donald Sutherland, but ultimately yet one more in what was now becoming another run of Connery failures.

If *The First Great Train Robbery* was a failure, then *Meteor* was a disaster. Coming on the tail end of the disaster movie craze of the mid-seventies, and caught up somewhere in the *Star Wars*-inspired science-fiction boom that superseded it, *Meteor* was the tale of the titular rock heading towards Earth and the all-star cast that attempts to prevent it hitting, led by Connery's Dr Paul Bradley. It was most definitely an opportunistic movie, and consequently little attention was paid to the script. It was hoped that the strength of the film would lie in the special effects. It didn't. 'They were diabolical,' Connery complained. 'Shit flying across the screen instead of meteors.' The public and the critics agreed, making *Meteor* one of the biggest flops of the decade, something that didn't reflect well on anyone associated with it. Perhaps the *New Statesman* said it best when it labelled the film 'Not so much a disaster movie as a disaster'.

Still, Connery did enjoy working in America again for the first time in many years, and even took the time to take martial arts lessons from Steven Segal, an instructor who would soon become a minor-league movie star in his own right.

Keeping his losing streak running at full steam, Connery saw out the decade with 1979's *Cuba*.

*Not a cigar in sight
– Connery with gun
in Richard Lester's
Cuba (1979)* ☆

Richard Lester, so pleased with their relationship and achievements on *Robin and Marian*, commissioned Charles Wood to pen the *Cuba* screenplay, with Connery specifically in mind for the lead role. The only problem was, he never stopped writing it. With Spain doubling for Cuba, it was essential weather-wise that the film start on time, meaning they went ahead with a half-finished script. 'I didn't think the script was ever ready,' Connery later said, 'so it became a patchwork. In my opinion Lester hadn't done his homework.'

The loss of promised government support to the production in the way of soldiers didn't help matters during the shoot, neither did the train that broke down, nor the plane that crashed before its scenes were complete. At one point Connery looked ready to leave the set. Maybe he should have done so, for the erratic, ill-conceived film that emerged did him no favours and only served to show that, after a brief, promising artistic resurgence in the middle of the decade, Sean Connery's career had been on a distinct downward spiral throughout the 1970s. 'I haven't made too many mistakes,' the actor reasoned, 'but I made one with *Cuba*.'

His two biggest hits of that decade had been *Murder on the Orient Express* and *A Bridge Too Far*, both of them ensemble pieces, neither of them particularly reliant on Connery in terms of drawing their audience. No doubt many of the movies Connery made in the late seventies were influenced by the realization that his business manager had left him considerably less well off than he believed himself to be. However, the need to build up finances had left him with a tarnished reputation as a movie star.

In terms of his career, Connery was lost. His recent attempts at strong leading-man roles had bombed, his option was to continue along the path he had tried to mine, that of an ageing character actor. But would that be enough? Certainly it wasn't enough to ensure a hit.

However by now there was a whole new generation of film-makers emerging in Hollywood. A generation for whom James Bond had been their introduction to, and definition of, masculinity. To them Connery was not a mere actor, he was an icon. They were making movies now – and they wanted Connery.

5. The Rediscovered Hero

Following the unwelcome experience of *Cuba*, Connery took eighteen months off from the big screen and bought a pig farm in Iowa. Not the obvious move for a man trying to reassess his career, but during this time Connery's mind was undoubtedly on matters more fiscal. The pig farm was a sound investment and, after recent events, here was a man who wanted to get his house in order.

He also parted ways with his London agent, signing with Michael Ovitz in the US instead, although he insisted that he would be personally involved in all of his future negotiations. 'He had quite obviously suffered a few heartfelt lessons,' his golfing friend Eric Sykes reckoned at the time. 'He made no secret of the fact that he had been taken for a few hard rides by some very clever international people. He now decided to be his own man and run everything himself – no managers, no hangers-on, just him and Micheline.'

Part of this action involved sorting out various litigious claims he had become involved in. He successfully sued the distributors of *The Man Who Would Be King*

A relatively hirsute Connery arrives at Heathrow airport, early 1980s ☆

for outstanding profits owed both to him and Michael Caine, in a precedent-setting case that had lasted three years. Additionally, he instigated legal action against Kenneth Richards, who had in turn decided to sue the actor for a share of his earnings for the period after Richards had been sacked.

The only talk of work was the rumour of Connery returning as Bond in Kevin McClory's long-delayed *Thunderball* remake, but when it became apparent that it was still bogged down in a number of legal wrangles, and given that Connery had a few outstanding lawsuits of his own on the go, he issued a statement backing away from the project. 'Plenty of people were wanting to contribute to the picture financially. There were no problems on that score. But I was under the impression that it was totally clean. Free from any litigational problems. When we started to talk quite seriously about the possibility it became so complex. The lawyers came out of the woodwork by the hundred. Then the publicity started to work on it and I said, "That's enough!" and walked away.'

Then again, never say never…

The hero reborn – Connery the great Greek–Scot – in Terry Gilliam's Time Bandits *(1981)* ☆

It was Terry Gilliam who first cast Connery as an iconic figure. The former Monty Python member was well aware of the power and baggage that Connery brought to the screen and, rather than deny it or try to avoid it, he embraced it, celebrated it even. Sean Connery was a hero, and what's more a hero of almost classical proportions. These times just didn't seem right for him, so Gilliam cast him in his fantasy adventure *Time Bandits*, as the Greek King, Agamemnon.

'We wrote in the script that when the Greek warrior removes his helmet he reveals himself to be none other than Sean Connery or an actor of equal but cheaper stature,' says Gilliam. 'It was just a joke. We had no idea that we'd ever get Sean Connery.'

Gilliam's producer Dennis O'Brien took the film-maker at his tongue-in-cheek word, and pursued Connery. Over a game of golf, Connery, a long-time Python fan, agreed to come on board. 'They sent me the script and said they couldn't possibly afford for me to do it. I liked the story so much – and they were having problems getting set-up – that I was determined to make a deal whatever way we worked it out.' Connery's decision to forgo payment in favour of a share of the profits proved to be a wise one when *Time Bandits* went on to become his biggest hit in years.

His scenes in the movie were partly shot on location in Morocco. These were the first days of the film's production and for Craig Warnock, who played the eight-year-old hero Kevin, his first days ever in front of a camera. Aware of the situation, Connery did all he could to help his director.

'It was the first day of shooting and there we were in this sweltering heat with Sean Connery and a boy who had never been in a movie before,' Gilliam later said, 'and I had this storyboard that would've taken about a week to shoot and I was trying to do it in one day. And Sean, the sensible man, the experienced man, said, "Forget about this. What you do is get me on the horse and get me out of here. And then you can spend time with the kid." He basically created a situation where I had to be totally pragmatic and not do what I was dreaming of doing, which was impossible. And that was absolutely vital to getting through those beginning days of the film. He's very canny, it takes time for him to develop trust in people – these are all good qualities and on that first day he didn't quite trust me. Which is fair enough, especially with the madness that was going on in my storyboard. The other great memories I have are of him sitting in these dusty little huts on location in Morocco, eating boxed lunches with the rest of us. He was just one of the team. And him telling stories of making *The Man Who Would Be King* in the same neighbourhood. He had just the right twinkle, the right amount of authority. Everything's there. We wanted a hero and Connery's a hero.'

In most other ensemble pieces, Connery had appeared as just one of the all-star turns, but here his presence, and the weight that came with it, was essential. So much so, that midway through production it was decided that Agamemnon needed to return at the end of the movie.

'We still needed something more at the end,' Gilliam says. 'And then I remembered during my first meeting with Sean, he'd talked about Agamemnon coming back at the end as the fireman and rescuing the kid at the end, having died in his dreams, he turns up in reality. We had already shot the firemen coming to rescue Kevin out of his bedroom. But we hadn't shot the very end scene outside the house. Actually we hadn't written that scene yet. Sean was coming back to England and I thought Jesus it would be great to get him back as a fireman. He was back in England for one day because of his tax-exile business. And he was meeting with his accountant, and from the meeting till lunch there was a gap, so we got him to drop by Lee studios in London. He turned up and all we had were fire trucks, there was no set, because we were just in the parking lot. And we did two shots – one with him putting Kevin down by the fire truck, and then another shot of him climbing into the cab and looking back and winking at him. And about a month or two later we went out and shot the rest of the scene.'

Gilliam was the first film-maker to rediscover the true heroic nature of Connery's screen appeal. He would not be the last, as over the coming years

High Noon *in space:*
armed and intergalactic
for Outland *(1981)*☆

Connery appeared in a number of fantasy and adventure movies that subtly redefined his screen image once again – this time into an increasingly patriarchal hero – and reaffirmed his status as one of the biggest movie stars in the world.

Peter Hyams had decided to remodel the classic western *High Noon*, for a science-fiction adventure called *Outland*. Connery was taking on the old Gary Cooper sheriff role – how could a man who had named himself after Shane possibly say no?

'I was certainly most conscious of the *High Noon* aspects when I read the script. I don't think Peter Hyams, in any way, ever tried to disguise the fact that it was based very heavily on *High Noon*. The situation, of course, is somewhat different, but the parallels and similarities are still there. What was clever, I think, was the idea of setting it in space – a frontier town. That's what appealed to me in the first place. Peter Hyams, who wrote the screenplay and was directing, was also heavily involved in the production design. Consequently, one was dealing

Connery with second
wife Micheline ☆

with the design and the dialogue at the same time when we started discussing the film. I liked his mix of western, science fiction, adventure and the sort of thriller in which one used computers, surveillance instruments that visually told the story.'

At Connery's suggestion, *Outland* was shot at Pinewood Studios, his first time shooting a full movie in London since 1974, although his tax status meant the film could not afford to run over schedule, with Connery only allowed ninety days of residence in the UK in any one year.

As ever, the actor had a hand in shaping the script. 'I work on all the scripts I film,' he said at the time, going on to explain further the form this involvement takes. 'I supply some ideas, changes in dialogue, and perhaps add any humour that's missing. From the moment I receive a script and become enthusiastic about it and say "Yes", the next step is to know if it's a definite offer. Because I've been caught many times where I've got involved and invested a lot of time and effort and realized too late that the film was not a possibility at all. Now I make it conditional that the moment I read and like the thing, and it's definite, I go to America to meet the writer or director or they come to see me where I'm filming and I go into the pre-production planning with him or them.'

'I found him to be very challenging,' said Peter Hyams, 'genuinely intelligent when it came to the screenplay. Sean made wonderful suggestions about motivations, and was ready to relinquish screen time if another actor's part needed development.'

Outland did not enjoy the success of many of its science-fiction contemporaries, but it was a powerful and important role for its lead actor. Connery brought an innate morality to his character. This image of the genuine hero alone in a world of anti-heroes, bemused more than angered at the morally uncertain world he sees around him, was to become a key part of his on-screen make-up for the next several years. He was often cast in roles in which this moral certainty, this knowledge, saw him as the patriarchal figure for a whole new generation of screen stars, waiting to be led by those who were wiser, those who had gone before them.

Uncharacteristically, Connery chose to make himself more available to the press than he had in years in promoting *Outland*, particularly at that year's Deauville Film Festival, which honoured him with a retrospective of his screen career, the first non-American to be honoured by this generally exclusively American event.

He also arranged for the European premiere of the film to be held in Edinburgh, the profits going to the Scottish International Education Trust, although he and his star guests – Ronnie Corbett and Bruce Forsyth among them – almost didn't make it to the show, when their flight to Scotland was grounded after a bomb scare and death threats against the actor. 'The whole thing is ridiculous, because I am neither political nor religious.'

Connery was clearly invigorated by his eighteen-month sabbatical and he threw himself into work, moving swiftly from *Outland* to America for the political satire/thriller *Wrong Is Right*. Once again, he was keen to lend his services to the script-doctoring department, especially given that writer-director Richard Brooks's script clocked in at around the 280-page mark, more than twice as long as was generally acceptable. 'He agreed I would assist with the cutting and reshaping of the script, which I did,' Connery explained. 'So we ended up with just the two of us having scripts. As I finished changes, I'd give the pages to him, so they wouldn't be xeroxed and sold or something. That was a very, very good working experience.'

Brooks's film was a vaguely futuristic look at the American media, the FBI, the CIA, and the shifting ground all these institutions were then inhabiting in the early days of mass-global communications. Connery took the lead role of an international TV reporter, a character the actor described as 'a kind of exalted Barbara Walters gone wrong'. It was a quirky, prescient film and, despite the sight of Sean Connery removing his toupée on camera for the first time, one that failed to find its audience in its day, even

when it was retitled *The Man with the Deadly Lens* and given a distinctly Bond-like poster design for its UK release.

Having starred in a future-vision remake of *High Noon*, Connery next got a chance to work with the director of that classic western, Fred Zinnemann. Fresh from his work on *Wrong Is Right*, Connery flew to Switzerland to begin two weeks of intense mountaineering training to star in Zinnemann's pet project, then titled *Maiden, Maiden*. Connery was to play the older man in a mountain-bound triangular love story.

Although the movie was clearly a labour of love for the director, and no one was expecting it to set the world on fire, working with the legendary film-maker was a joy for Connery. 'The number of films he's made isn't many, but the spectrum is very wide and quite diverse. I spent a lot of time talking with him, because the script is very episodic, just page or page-and-a-half scenes, and what's going to be important, I think, is what lies between or beneath the lines. Fred is an incredible man who just loves the mountains. His idea of heaven is to be stuck up the Matterhorn and not know the way down.'

Filming of what was to become *Five Days One Summer* also took Connery back to Scotland. It was one of the rare opportunities he'd had to film in his homeland.

Connery in the little-seen satire, Wrong Is Right *(aka* The Man with the Deadly Lens, *1982)* ☆

At this time, late 1981, the Connerys' long-gestating legal case against former business manager Kenneth Richards finally found its way to the High Court. Richards's case fell apart under cross-examination and the court found in favour of Connery's claim. The actor was clearly upset by the whole experience, explaining to reporters outside the court, 'When people read that I was near to tears at the announcement of the verdict they don't recognize the significance of my counter-claim against Mr Richards. His claim was for a trivial sum compared to what he owes me, and now it is up to the court to decide the amount.'

He was initially awarded a million pounds to be paid by Richards, but Connery doubted he would ever see his money again. This was confirmed months later when a final award of £2.8 million was reached, and Richards declared himself bankrupt shortly after.

He was quick, however, to see money from *The Sword of the Valiant*, a sword-and-sorcery mini-epic, based on the legend of Sir Gawain and the Green Knight, made for those exploitation masters of the early eighties, Cannon Films. 'The material is stimulating and interesting,' he said in defence of his choice, which only required him to shoot for a handful of days. 'A kind of morality tale.' It was by no means a worthy addition to his back catalogue, not even warranting a theatrical release.

Connery's next move was possibly the strangest of his entire career. He decided to play James Bond again. From the off, he had viewed Bond as a potential millstone, which proved to be the case from the first preview of *Shalako* onwards. There had been many moments of artistic achievement away from 007, most notably his historical trilogy of the mid-seventies, and many subtle shifts in how he presented himself and how he was perceived. By the early eighties he finally seemed to be finding the right niche for himself, mapping out the territory of the heroic, slightly older leading man. To go back to being Bond said what exactly? That he had lost his way? That he was still aggrieved with his former producers (against who he would soon launch another major lawsuit)? That he was simply in it for the money (which was considerable)?

Whatever Connery's ultimate motivations – and in interviews at the time he was deliberately evasive – it turned out to be one of his most astute and successful moves.

Kevin McClory had finally won his legal action against Cubby Broccoli in 1980, but this time found himself without funds. The best way to get a James Bond movie off the ground was, of course, to secure the presence of Sean Connery in the lead role. With Roger Moore then being offered $4 million for the upcoming official Bond movie *Octopussy*, Connery was offered – and accepted – $5 million. After

Back as Bond, with new girl Kim Basinger – Never Say Never Again (1983) ☆

having backtracked once again on the issue of donning secret-agent regulation tux and shoulder holster, it was Micheline Connery who suggested the title of the movie, her tongue firmly in her cheek – *Never Say Never Again*.

Indeed, Connery credited his wife with persuading him to return to Her Majesty's fold. 'My wife Micheline encouraged me to think about it carefully. "Why not play the role? What would you risk? After all these years it might be interesting." The more I thought about it, the more I felt she was right. There was also a certain amount of curiosity in me about the role, having been so long away from it.'

Although Connery had worked on a version of the script with Len Deighton, ex-*Batman* scribe Lorenzo Semple Jr was hired to pen the screenplay, with Connery, as ever, involving himself in the process, roping in British sitcom stalwarts Dick Clement and Ian La Frenais (who would often work uncredited on Connery's material over the coming years). Irvin Kershner, who had directed Connery way back in 1966's *A Fine Madness*, and, more recently, had had a major triumph with the second instalment of the *Star Wars* saga, *The Empire Strikes Back*, was brought on board as director.

In interviews to promote the movie, Connery was – for once – eager to associate himself with the role, perhaps as spoiler for the Roger Moore

Connery with long-time friend Roger Moore, who when once asked how his performance as James Bond differed from the Scot's, replied 'My teeth are whiter.' ☆

adventure, both of which were scheduled to open against each other in the summer of 1983.

'I'm naturally cool, which I suppose is a help when playing Bond,' the actor stated. 'I use as much of myself as possible to make the role work. Basically, I begin from the reality of the situation – in any part I play. Then I try to extract the humour from the character because, for me, those aspects are much more interesting and revealing – and harder to play – then all the melodramatic stuff. The dramatics take care of themselves if you get it right. The humour you have to find.'

Complete with Klaus Maria Brandauer on board as the Bond villain, Kim Basinger and Barbara Carrera as the requisite Bond girls, Max von Sydow giving us his Blofeld, Bernie Casey standing in as an African-American Felix Leiter and Edward Fox signing on as M, *Never Say Never Again* began filming on location in the suitably glamorous South of France in September 1982. It was not to be an easy shoot, with Connery increasingly incensed at what he saw as the lack of support and effort on the part of the producer. 'All kinds of shit was flying,' he said, shortly after completing the film. 'Quite frankly, I could have just taken an enormous amount of money and walked away from the whole thing and the picture would never have been finished. I could have let it bury itself, but once I was in there, I found myself in the middle of every decision. Myself and the assistant director produced that picture.'

Despite the problems during filming, *Never Say Never Again* provided all the essential elements of the classic Bond movies and proved a huge hit upon its release the following summer (although Moore's effort beat it at the US box office – $37 to $35 million – something that undoubtedly annoyed Connery), with critics eager to welcome the actor back to his defining role.

Connery had returned to his old stomping ground, on his own terms and proved himself a success, with the film becoming a global box-office triumph, even if it did tail behind *Octopussy*. If truth be told, *Never Say Never Again* was an entertaining Bond romp, decent enough by the standards of the day, but then again the standards of the day were the lowest in the history of the official Bond franchise.

What Connery had achieved more than anything with the movie was to play Bond as a man in his mid fifties, older certainly, wiser, not really, but still more than up to the job. A credible, middle-aged hero, with sex appeal to spare and a pan-global appeal. The movie world took notice.

6. The Father Figure

'I have this theory – and it's just my own opinion – but I think that somehow the idea of playing this surrogate father Agamemnon appealed to him, just because of whatever he was feeling about his own family life.' – Terry Gilliam, director of *Time Bandits*.

Whatever Sean Connery chose to be, he wanted to be the best at it. If there was a race to be run, he was going to make damn sure he was the winner. While his contemporaries were prepared to go head-to-head with the younger generation of leading men who had followed in their wake, Connery simply acknowledged the fact that he was now fifty-five and recast himself in another role. Having reconfirmed his presence as an iconic screen hero, Connery cannily lent his name, talent and stature to a host of young pretenders to the crown, ennobling them in the process and consolidating his status along the way.

'There are two different modes of acting old,' he once explained. 'One, which is wonderful, is where you get someone like Lillian Gish, and everyone says isn't she

Connery triumphant –
Best Supporting Actor
Oscar for 1987's The
Untouchables ☆

The immortal Spanish-monikered, Egyptian-born, Scottish-accented Juan Ramirez proves himself a superior swordsman, Highlander *(1986)* ☆

marvellous, she's ninety-two, or whatever. The other way is to acknowledge your age, and the approach of death, and incorporate it into whatever you do. This whole era can hardly come to terms with death.'

Thus, the screen image of Connery the sexy father figure was born, a role he would play for the next several years opposite such actors as Kevin Costner, Harrison Ford, Christian Slater, Alec Baldwin, Christopher Lambert, Richard Gere and Nicolas Cage, even Dustin Hoffman, who was in fact only seven years his junior.

Playing this role for the next decade or more would bring Connery his greatest successes, including the ultimate seal of Hollywood approval, in the form of an Oscar win – and on his very first nomination.

The first movie in this cycle sounded perfect for the world's most famous Scot. It was a surprise then for audiences to learn that in the fantasy adventure *Highlander*, Connery played an Egyptian immortal with a Spanish name, Juan Ramirez (complete with Scottish accent, of course).

'When I first read the *Highlander* script,' Connery recalled, 'I thought it was an interesting idea to give someone all the time in the world. If you work it out Ramirez is about 2,766 years old and he would have been exposed to all these different cultures and what have you. It was a challenge to imbue him with as much of the cultural aspects he would obviously have come into contact with. The character was eloquent and humorous, a man of the world, and very much the teacher. The humour came out of things he wouldn't know about in certain areas – there's a scene in *Highlander* when I'm on a boat with Christopher and he says, "What's your game, shithead?" Well, if you think about it, what is a shithead? That sort of humour was the most important element in the film as far as I was concerned.'

For the seven days he spent pondering the nature of a shithead, the actor was paid $1 million, and when director Russell Mulcahy asked him to rehearse the film's numerous sword fights ahead of time, it cost him another $10,000. Connery, convinced his fencing skills were up to scratch, flew to the location by helicopter, disembarked, picked up a sword and a handy stuntman opponent, and called out 'One thousand' on the first thrust, 'Two thousand' on the next, all the way up to ten, then he hopped back on the chopper and was gone, laughing, quite literally, all the way to the bank.

Nonetheless, the actor's bravado appeared misplaced when he was mildly injured in a sword fight on his first day of filming, leading him to explode at his director. 'He went apeshit and started screaming. So I said, "Well it's your fault. You refused to come in and do any bloody rehearsals. What do you expect? You're going to get cut, aren't you?"'

For the remainder of his few days on the picture, Connery took to rehearsing his fight moves behind his trailer during lunch breaks. 'I think it was more pride than anything else,' Mulcahy said, 'because the whole crew was there when the man fucked up.' Mulcahy also recalled how the crew would be subjected to what they called 'Connery Meetings' when the actor would group everyone together and air his views on what he thought was and wasn't working. 'This was free advice – very expensive free advice,' Mulcahy recalled.

Surprisingly, *Highlander* proved to be a resounding flop at the American box office, but it went on to become a huge cult hit in Europe, spawning hit records, sequels and, eventually, a TV series.

While happily cutting a dash on screens all round Europe, Connery was also keeping a proud eye on his son Jason, who had decided to follow his father into the profession and was now finding great success for himself on television. With a fitting sense of irony, he was playing a younger version of a character his father had played at the end of that character's life – starring in the title role of *Robin of Sherwood*.

In an unexpected move, Connery took a short break from the screen, in favour of radio. Some enterprising producer at the BBC was setting up a production of *After the Fire*, a short play by Peter Barnes, and had decided that his dream cast would be Donald Pleasence, John Hurt and Sean Connery.

On little more than a whim and profound hope, an offer was sent out to Connery to come and make his radio-acting debut. Much to everyone's surprise, he accepted, even allowing for the fact that he would have to fly over from Spain for the fifteen-minute piece at his own expense. In addition, he donated his nominal fee from the broadcast to the Scottish International Education Trust.

Still in a charitable mood, when Connery read of the potential closure of the National Youth Theatre in London, due to an Arts Council cut of £100,000, he promptly dashed off a cheque for the first £50,000 with his best wishes that this venerable institution continue.

His next movie saw Connery once again in period costume, and once again mentoring a younger star. In *The Name of the Rose*, Jean-Jacques Annaud's adaptation of Umberto Eco's international best-seller, Connery played William of Baskerville, a fourteenth-century Franciscan monk, investigating a murder at a remote monastery, with the assistance of his young novice, Christian Slater.

Annaud had originally wanted Michael Caine for the lead role 'but the day I had a meeting with Connery suddenly he was there. Sean has only to say maybe and he's beautiful.'

Filming in sub-zero temperatures in monasteries in Frankfurt and Stuttgart, Connery cited *The Name of the Rose* as the most difficult shoot he'd ever been on, remarking on set, 'I'm wearing a monk's outfit, thermal underwear and space boots and my arse is still freezing. You could hang meat on this set.'

Back in the studio at Rome's Cinecittà, evening dinners between the actor and his director became a regular occurrence, where Connery would entertain the other guests by doing magic tricks and singing Spanish songs, while his director danced the flamenco.

Eliciting one of Connery's best performances, the film was an astonishing success in Europe, taking over $100 million at the Euro-box office. Connery became vocal, however, when this success was not repeated in America. '*The Name of the Rose* has taken more money in West Germany than in the whole of America,' he said at the time, 'and that's because they don't know how to market the picture. They just trot it out, without thinking of the right time, the right climate, the right sort of cinema, and they have dumped on it. The other problem of course is that *The Name of the Rose* is dealing with a period of history before America existed. In America they have all been weaned on vitamins since the Revolution and they all look wonderful. Here's this film full of medieval monks, who look hideous, like gargoyles, and I don't think they can take it.'

Playing father figure to Christian Slater's novice monk, The Name of the Rose (1986) ☆

Andy Garcia, Robert De Niro, Charles Martin Smith, Kevin Costner and Sean Connery step out for The Untouchables' premiere, 1987 ☆

Despite, or perhaps in spite of the movie's lack of success Stateside, *The Name of the Rose* proved to be an extremely significant film in Connery's career. It appeared at a time when cinema in general was changing, in that the US, always perceived to be any movie's main market, was now being matched and often out-paced by the rest of the world market. It was now possible to have a major-hit movie, even if the film did little or no business in America, and Connery, being tremendously popular globally (*The Name of the Rose* knocked *Highlander* off the top spot at the European box office), benefited greatly as this trend continued unabated over the next decade and more.

Had the American distributor marketed *The Name of the Rose* successfully, it might well have garnered an Oscar nomination for Connery, something he had yet to achieve; this was a long-standing matter that was to be addressed with his next movie.

Although adapted from a ropy old television show, *The Untouchables*, in the hands of flamboyant director Brian De Palma and screenwriter David Mamet, became a thing of beauty. A moral epic that pitched Armani-clad cops against tuxedo-wearing, baseball-bat-wielding gangsters. And the Connery-as-father-figure persona was never more pronounced than in his role as Jimmy Malone, an incorruptible veteran beat cop turned wise old sage to Kevin Costner's naive yet passionate Eliot Ness. In Costner, Connery found the perfect reflection of his younger self – a talented actor, a serious sex symbol and above all, a man prepared to cut through the crap, walk his own path, and show Hollywood exactly what the definition of a 'star' was.

Shooting began in August 1986, with De Palma encouraging Connery's mentor position with the young cast off camera as well as on. 'I kept them very much on a wire by snide little remarks, digs at America, what have you.' It was all good-natured – even when Connery would go up to Costner after a take and say, 'Is that the best it's going to get?' – and helped to build the rapport of the team. Although impressed with the calibre of Mamet's script, Connery did feel obliged to offer one contribution, in the scene where Malone explains the Chicago way to his young moral apprentice. 'I thought it should be done in a church,' he said.

'When you're making that kind of declaration about the Chicago way – you know, "Capone puts one of yours in the hospital, you put one of his in the morgue" – all this kind of dialogue, if you put it in a church, it suddenly becomes something different.'

Another defining sequence in *The Untouchables* was also arrived at late in the day. The original climax was to have taken place on board a speeding train, but as De Palma ran over-budget, there was no money left to shoot it. So the highly inventive director improvised the film's incredible, nail-biting final shoot-out in Union Station, and chucking in a homage to the Odessa steps sequence from Eisenstein's *Battleship Potemkin* for extra good measure.

Costner later recalled one amusing moment from the shoot. 'I remember one night when he really got me. I was talking about my favourite movie in the world, *Hombre*, and I was doing it to the nth detail, doing all the parts, all the voices and finally I say, "Then this bitch gets in front of Paul Newman and she won't move. The bitch ends up getting him killed." And Sean just looks at me and says, "That bitch was my first wife."'.

The Untouchables opened to eulogistic reviews and ringing cash registers, becoming a major international hit. Along the way, there was the constant rumour that this was Connery's year, and awards season was just a few short months away.

There promptly followed a BAFTA nomination, a Golden Globe win and – the big one – the Academy Award for Best Supporting Actor, presented to Connery along with a rapturous reception from his peers.

The Untouchables was the movie that solidly placed Connery back in the Hollywood firmament. Now Hollywood seemed to know what to do with him, and although his next movie, *The Presidio*, a below-par military thriller, was a brief side-step in the wrong direction, its box-office takings did show that audiences were only too willing to stand in line now to see Sean Connery. And there was considerably better than *The Presidio* on the way.

Just who do you get to play Indiana Jones's dad? Well, an old James Bond, naturally.

Devised by George Lucas and directed by Steven Spielberg, the *Indiana Jones* movies, starring Harrison Ford, were inspired by the Saturday-morning serials of yore. But more than anything, they owed their structure to the Bond movies. Each *Indiana* adventure began with a startling pre-credit sequence, that saw the intrepid archaeologist/adventurer wrapping up his previous adventure in grand style, before returning home to learn of his next adventure. Many exotic locations and the occasional gorgeous woman peppered the action from there on in.

The first two instalments had proved enormously successful, and for the third and possibly final episode in the series, *Indiana Jones and the Last Crusade*, Spielberg and Lucas had decided to introduce the progenitor of this latter-day movie hero. It was De Palma who tipped Spielberg's hand when he showed him a rough cut of *The Untouchables*. Besides, who else could fit the bill but Sean Connery, the man who had, in his way, given birth to all the screen-action heroes who had followed him.

Lucas was at first reluctant to cast Connery, while Connery at first was reluctant to take the role. 'George wasn't thinking in terms of such a powerful presence,' explained Spielberg. 'His idea was for a doting, scholarly person, an older British character. But I had always seen Sean Connery. Without a strong illuminating presence, I was afraid that Harrison Ford would eradicate the father from the movie. I wanted to challenge him. And who could be the equal of Indiana Jones but James Bond.'

Connery's initial misgivings about taking on the role of Dr Henry Jones were down to the script. Jones Sr was initially more of a marginal presence, not appearing until later in the film. It was Connery's notion to introduce him earlier, involve him more in the action, and make him the sexual equal of his son, in one of the film's funniest moments, when both men discover that they have

With co-star Mark Harmon in publicity shot for The Presidio *(1988)* ☆

been the recent lovers of female lead Alison Doody.

Connery envisaged the character more as a Victorian eccentric, his performance being influenced in part by his vision of Sir Richard Burton, the explorer whose life he had tried to bring to the screen back in the seventies.

'Sean thought Dr Jones was too much like a doddering Yoda character,' said his co-star Harrison Ford. 'So he went to work and gave the character a charm and a wit and the energy that is all Sean.'

Spielberg was equally pleased by the contributions Connery had to offer. 'Sean was instrumental in all the rewrites. And when he has a good idea, which is about twenty times a day, he's such a child, his face lights up.'

Filming began in May 1988 in a variety of locations ranging from America to Germany to Venice to Jordan. The chemistry between Connery and Ford was instant and abundant and Connery rated the production as one of the happiest of his career. One day while filming a father-and-son discussion in close-up in 100-degree-plus heat, Connery decided to cool himself down by dropping his out-of-shot trousers. Ford, initially unsure of such drastic measures, soon followed suit as the sweat continued to pour.

The movie was released in summer 1989 and rapidly became Sean Connery's biggest hit ever. Although his was technically the supporting role,

Steven Spielberg directs father-and-son act, Connery and Harrison Ford, in Indiana Jones and the Last Crusade *(1989)* ☆

critics and audiences generally agreed that he stole the movie from his leading man, as he had done in both *Highlander* and *The Untouchables* before.

Having sired Ford, twelve years his junior, Connery then went on to play father to Dustin Hoffman, a mere seven years younger, in the thick-as-thieves drama *Family Business*. (For good measure, he also played grandfather to rising Hollywood talent Matthew Broderick.) Once again,

Connery was lured by the attraction of working with director Sidney Lumet, this their fifth collaboration. Lumet was adamant that the only man for the patriarchal role of Jessie McMullen was Connery. 'Jessie needed to be an attractive role model to his grandson, and I really don't know of any other actor who could have played him with so much charm and charisma,' said the director of his leading man.

Taking this father figure thing too far? Connery with Dustin Hoffman, seven years his junior, Family Business *(1989)* ☆

As ever, Connery involved himself with the scriptwriter Vincent Patrick, aiming to remove some of the softer edges from the character.

Hoffman and Connery were old friends, but Broderick remained a little in awe of the elder statesman during filming, although when Connery wasn't around, he was quick to let people hear his Connery-as-Bond impersonation. When Connery heard about it, he asked why the young actor never did the impression for him: he was told Broderick was too afraid. 'Good,' he replied, 'he should be.'

Remarkably, given the talent involved, *Family Business* was a flop at the box office. 'I would've assumed people would have gone to it just out of curiosity,' said a surprised Connery. But they didn't. 'A film when it is finished is like a young bird leaving the nest,' he philosophized at the time. 'Once out, it's up to the bird to fly around or fall on

Calling the shots in the 1990s – The Hunt For Red October ☆

its arse. But if you believed in it in the first place then it doesn't matter.'

It was during the filming of *Family Business* that Connery became aware of some problems with his throat. At first he thought it was laryngitis, but a trip to the doctor revealed it to be a small growth of polyps on his vocal chords. After three second opinions, Connery found himself faced with the prospect of minor surgery, something he dreaded, or not speaking for thirty days. Connery opted for silence.

He walked around with a card that read *I'm sorry, I cannot speak. I have a problem with my throat. Thank you* and a pad to write any further answers on. He despaired when others used this pad to ask their questions of him. 'You realize very quickly that the world is full of idiots,' he said of the experience. 'I wrote hundreds of pages and I should have kept them because it was so crazy. It was lots of non sequiturs, because you never knew the question. Like there would be, "How the fuck do I know?"'

Thirty days later, the silent treatment hadn't worked, and Connery was forced to undergo the surgery. The tabloid press latched on to the event and – wrongly – started rumours of cancer. The scare-mongering continued, and increased when the polyps reappeared. Connery this time underwent radiation treatment, fuelling the cancer scares, and fully recovered.

It was of course, a great worry that anything could damage Connery's instantly recognizable voice. After all, who else could get away with playing a Russian submarine captain with the most famous Scottish burr in the world? For that was exactly what Connery did in his next film, *The Hunt for Red October*. Based on the bestselling techno-thriller by Tom Clancy, Connery was offered the lead role of Soviet submarine Captain Marko Raimus after Klaus Maria Brandauer had dropped out. At first however, the actor rejected the script, saying that, in light of recent political events, it was now outdated. It transpired that the first page of the script – which explained that the story was set in a pre-glasnost era – was missing from Connery's copy. When he was informed of this, he reconsidered and readily signed aboard, for a not inconsiderable fee of $4 million. (He cannily had his agent negotiate compensation on this fee if the dollar fell against European currencies – 'I don't think the studio had heard that argument

before, but funnily enough they came round to my way of thinking.')

Cast opposite Alec Baldwin, Connery began his involvement in the film by hiring John Milius to rewrite his role. He then designed the look of the character, seeing Raimus as a mixture of Stalin and Samuel Beckett, with a military brush of hair and an austere white beard.

'The minute he stepped on the set he became unapproachable,' said director John McTiernan, complimenting his actor on imbuing the character with just the right level of authority. 'Everyone else around him involuntarily straightened up.'

At one point, dismayed by the amount of chaos he saw on the production, Connery took action and had the set closed down. 'I said, "I'm not going to work in this climate." We closed the set down on a Monday, we rehearsed and blocked everything. Then we'd go and get made up, change, and whenever it was all ready, we'd come back and do a rehearsal for everyone. And then we'd get on the stage – we, the actors and director – and we'd do it till we were happy. I don't find inefficiency bad if it's the outcome of enthusiasm. But movies are decisions, everybody has to make decisions.'

McTiernan ultimately did a splendid job in bringing Clancy's tension-building clash-of-ideologies drama to the screen, and Connery delivered one of his most effective performances.

The film proved to be a major worldwide success, which, along with the recent *Indiana Jones* triumph, placed Connery firmly in the blockbuster division. At the time of its release, the star ruminated on the position in which he now found himself in Hollywood. 'I have enough power in terms of casting approval and director approval,' he said. 'But I don't think it's something someone can brandish like a sword. I sense myself as much more a responsible film-maker in terms of what's good for the overall picture, and for the actors as well, because I have had all this experience, and I've seen a lot of waste.'

One of the most important facts in Connery's re-emergence in Hollywood was undoubtedly his choice of agent. For years Connery had been represented by Brit Dennis Selinger, also the rep for Michael Caine and Peter Sellers, but in February 1979, Connery had decided that what he needed was a Hollywood agent. He signed with Michael Ovitz, then just starting out with a company called CAA (Creative Artists Agency). During the eighties, Ovitz would rise to become the most powerful agent in Hollywood; he got there in part, by trading on the name of his first major client, Sean Connery.

'The best thing Sean ever did,' says former Bond director Terence Young, 'was returning Michael Ovitz's call. Believe me, Michael Ovitz is the most important man in Sean's life.'

Romancing Michelle Pfeiffer, The Russia House *(1990)* ☆

In 1990, Connery held a star-studded bash to celebrate his sixtieth birthday. Shortly before this momentous occasion, the actor received a present he wasn't expecting. *People* magazine voted him the recipient of their annual 'Sexiest Man Alive' honour. At the ripe old age of sixty, Connery acted a touch bemused by the title, but in a strange way, more than anything, this tabloid honour was evidence that what he was doing was working. By this acknowledgement, Connery knew he had achieved what he set out to do. It showed that leading men could have a shelf-life, that sex appeal was not just the province of this year's flavour. While the Oscar and his continual high standard of work showed that Connery had matured as an actor, this curiously displayed how his innate appeal had not been diminished. No *On Golden Pond* for him. Connery was as vital now as he'd ever been. Still, he had the decency to act embarrassed for the rest of us. 'It's very flattering. But the sexiest man alive? There are few dead sexy ones.' Connery's impact as an actor had always been linked to his sex appeal. Key moments in his career had been inadvertently directed to it. He landed the role in *Requiem for a Heavyweight* in part on the advice of the director's wife who found him attractive; Cubby Broccoli's wife similarly pushed her husband to cast him as Bond. At sixty, it was obviously satisfying to realize that he wasn't out of the race; he was winning it.

Shelley Winters summed it up best in her open appreciation of all things Connery: 'He was sexy at twenty-six and at sixty even more so. He makes a woman feel sexual chemistry. To be his leading lady, I'd lose fifty pounds and get my face lifted. As a matter of fact, I'd get everything lifted.'

The ongoing appeal of Connery's innate virility was obviously a key factor in his next role, cast opposite Michelle Pfeiffer in an adaptation of John Le Carré's *The Russia House*. Like *The Hunt for Red October*, it was another movie with a Russian setting and theme, this time exploring life after glasnost, and who better to do that than the man who had helped define the Cold War.

Connery's importance to the project showed just how powerful his position in the movie world had now become. As director Fred Schepisi recalls, despite the fact it was adapted from an international best-seller and had Michelle Pfeiffer attached, 'The backers told us that we either got Sean or we could forget about the film. So I gave him the script, talked like hell and tried to convince him to do it. When you are looking for an actor who is big in both Europe and America, all roads lead to Sean.'

The Russia House offered the attraction of Connery making his first foray back into the spy movie since the days of Bond, and the potential heat generated by the teaming of the sexiest man alive and Michelle Pfeiffer, herself no slouch in the sex-appeal department. Yet the cold of its Moscow locations cooled the whole thing down and Connery once again found himself with a box-office failure on his hands.

But then a curious thing happened – it simply didn't matter.

Throughout the nineties, Connery's star appeal could not be dented by the public or critical response to any of his movies. The resurgence of his career, the respect of his peers, the support of the audience placed Connery in an exalted place. No matter how many disappointments he was associated with, he remained the real deal, a genuine movie star, incapable of being diminished by lack of box office. Perhaps it was the fact that even in a bad movie, he was always the best thing there, or perhaps it was the power of his personality and the associative memories it brought of so many great movies. Either way, Sean Connery didn't make a significant film for the next six years. And it didn't matter.

In the eight movies that followed, Connery vacillated between playing father figure to yet more young contenders, provided certain projects with little more than cameo appearances, and, in one case, when cast as a dragon, merely let the most recognizable (and most imitated) voice in movies do the work for him.

Up a tree with Lorraine Bracco, Medicine Man *(1992)* ☆

His brief end-of-movie appearance in 1991's *Robin Hood: Prince of Thieves* was primarily a gesture of friendship aimed at the star of the movie, his *Untouchables* partner Kevin Costner. Costner's reasoning had been that if Richard the Lionheart was to show up in the last thirty seconds, you needed an actor of sufficient stature to compete with the movie's previous two hours of action. Once again, who else could suffice but Connery?

He quickly followed this with ten days' work in Buenos Aires, reprising his role as Ramirez in *Highlander II – The Quickening*. An opportunistic sequel: one can't help but feel the $3 million for two weeks payday had something to do with his recreating his role.

The eco-theme of *Highlander II* was echoed in Connery's next film, *Medicine Man*. As with many a project, it was Connery's fascination with the theme – this time an exploration of the rainforest and a protagonist who believes he has found a natural cure for cancer there, but must work against the developers and devastation of the environment to bring his studies to the world – that excited and attracted the actor.

As with several other movies that had done the same – *Wrong Is Right*, *Zardoz*, etc. – the movie, which re-teamed Connery with *Red October* director John McTiernan, never really came together, with much talk of on-set in-fighting.

Connery himself described the movie as 'probably the worst experience of my life'.

It was, however, the first time that he took an Executive Producer credit on any of his films, finally and publicly acknowledging all the work he inevitably did off screen on the movies he was involved in.

Similarly attempting to catch the zeitgeist was 1993's *Rising Sun*, a sort of re-teaming with Michael Crichton, upon whose timely novel this tale of American–Japanese relations was based. The movie was a voguish thriller, which saw Connery once again playing wise old mentor, this time to Wesley Snipes. With his new distinguished grey hairpiece, Connery cut a fine figure and the movie did well at the box office, but, like much of Crichton's writings in the nineties, it was very much rooted in the issues of the day, and ultimately suffered from a plot more concerned with those issues than characterization.

Connery moved back into elongated cameo mode with William Boyd's *A Good Man in Africa*. The actor had long expressed his desire to appear in a farcical comedy. Sadly, this wasn't it. Still, the golf on location in South Africa (as seen in the movie) was remarkably good, so the movie wasn't a complete waste of time for Connery. The *Observer* newspaper summed it up best: 'By comparison, *Carry On Up the Khyber* is a satirical masterwork.'

Wesley Snipes,
Harvey Keitel and the
Zen-like Connery,
Rising Sun (1993) ☆

This was quickly followed by *Just Cause*, in which Connery played a Harvard law professor called to the South to save the life of a young black man on death row. It was as pedestrian as that brief plot summary makes it sound.

The actor's next appearance, as King Arthur in 1995's *First Knight* (and after a lifetime interest in Arthurian legend how could he pass on playing King Arthur?), felt like another protracted cameo,

while only his voice was required for the role of Draco, the last remaining computer-animated dragon in 1996's *Dragonheart*. Naturally, it was a Scottish dragon.

Rob Cohen, director of the latter, encouraged his digital animators to base their dragon's physical movements and expressions on Connery's own, assembling a wide variety of scenes from the actor's back catalogue to assist the animators. 'For

The women keep getting younger – with Julia Ormond, Guinevere to Connery's King Arthur, First Knight (1995) ☆

example, if we needed Draco to look angry, I could tell the animators, "Go to the anger bin and you will see something Sean does in *The Russia House* suitable for Draco in this moment."'

The Rock, however, was different. In many respects, this all-out action adventure summer blockbuster from producer Jerry Bruckheimer, was a ground-breaking film. It established the previously left-of-centre Nicolas Cage as a major action hero; it then recast the action hero, not as the muscle-bound excess of Stallone and Schwarzenegger, but as the semi-wimpy desk-bound ordinary man trapped in an extraordinary situation, in this case an attempt to break into world-famous prison Alcatraz – the 'Rock' – to stop a renegade group of soldiers unleashing a deadly chemical weapon on to San Francisco.

More than any movie since *The Untouchables*, *The Rock* found Connery perfectly cast in an iconic manner, his history and baggage wholly appropriate to the role – his John Mason, was a British spy, who in this case had spent the last thirty years illegally incarcerated by the CIA. Connery, with flowing grey locks, played the part to perfection, acting as both mentor figure to Cage's inexperienced sidekick, while once again asserting himself as a vital heroic figure. Never mind the age, feel the action.

Filmed on location in the now closed-down prison itself, *The Rock* was a hugely successful film on every level. A taut script, Cage playing wonderfully against type (reinventing the public's perception of him in the process) and novice Michael Bay's tight direction and unrelenting editing, combined to make a top-line summer movie. The action movie, more than any other genre, continually upped the stakes in the nineties. *The Rock* was an example of extreme, excessive film-making; it was also hugely entertaining. And at the centre of it all, providing a calm in the midst of all this MTV-inspired chaos, was Sean Connery, in his best role of the nineties. It was noise, he was silence, the very image of a master at work.

The film, released in 1996, was a huge global success earning over $300 million worldwide, making it one of Connery's biggest hits ever. It was a nice way to see in his new position as a pensioner. A Scottish bus company took the opportunity of this momentous occasion to send him his free old-age pensioner's bus pass. Connery replied, 'Many thanks for my bus pass. I don't know how many times I shall get the opportunity to use it, but I shall have it clutched to my bosom and I won't venture over the border without it.'

It wasn't just bus passes that Connery was picking up in the nineties. Fuelled by the 1987 Oscar win, it seemed everyone was queuing up to give the man an award.

October 1990 saw Connery surrounded by his colleagues and peers at the Odeon Leicester Square in London as the British Academy of Film and Television Arts gave him the prestigious Tribute Award, and the likes of son Jason, Kevin Costner and, gushing away, Dickie Attenborough, sang the star's praises.

'I've had a thirty-year filmic odyssey and met some marvellous people,' the obviously moved Connery stated. 'But what became apparent watching this evening was that I had not seen them as much as I should have.'

The National Association of Theatre Owners in America followed suit in 1991, devising a special award – Worldwide Star of the Year – making Sean Connery its inaugural recipient.

Even more important to the actor in 1991 was being awarded the Freedom of Edinburgh. Connery returned to his home town for the ceremony, held in a packed Edinburgh Usher Hall, on 11 June of that year.

Big Tam, who had sensed there was something more out there in the world, had gone away, conquered what he saw and returned triumphant. In introducing him to the gathered crowds, compère Tom Conti said, 'There are good actors who will never be stars. There are some stars who will never be actors. There are very, very few who, like Sean Connery, are both.'

Connery was visibly moved by the many tributes paid to him that night, none more so than by that of his old school friend Craig Veitch. 'Men who make it big often have their name linked to a region. Lawrence of Arabia, Scott of the Antarctic, Clive of India. Tonight, we have Connery of Edinburgh.'

The following July Connery was honoured by the American Cinemateque for his 'significant contribution to contemporary film'. Audrey Hepburn did the honours (six months before her untimely death).

The National Board of Review bestowed a lifetime achievement gong on him in 1994, while a similar award came his way in 1996, courtesy of the Hollywood Foreign Press Association.

In May 1997, he was honoured once more by the Film Society of Lincoln Center in New York. The BAFTA Fellowship followed in April 1998, and Connery saw out the century in December 1999 under the gaze of President Bill Clinton, when he was honoured once more by the Kennedy Center for the Performing Arts in Washington.

Connery was a hero. He always had been on screen. Even when playing flawed characters, with a few exceptions, part of Connery's appeal had always been linked to the nobility and heroism he so seamlessly projects. Perhaps that explains his

Best role of the nineties, worst hair of the nineties – Connery and Cage, The Rock (1996) ☆

Finally a chance to play a villain – August DeWynter tries on the charm with Emma Peel, The Avengers (1998) ☆

decision to play a villain. Nothing wrong in that, of course, it was just unfortunate that he chose to highlight his dark side in the lamentable big-screen adaptation of the cult, ultra-stylish 1960s television show, *The Avengers*. In a film in which nearly every single moment is misjudged and botched, Connery played August de Wynter, deranged meteorologist extraordinaire.

Obviously for the film's producer, Jerry Weintraub, it was a casting coup – landing one of the sixties' greatest icons for a remake of one of the sixties' most iconic shows, but one that Connery was quick to dismiss. 'This film is set at a time when there was no James Bond, the Beatles, Carnaby Street, and it's kind of hip and flip. It's a Magritte painting, a surrealistic world.'

Connery claims to have had his usual full input into the script. This is surprising inasmuch as he never seemed to notice how totally bad the script was. 'One of the conditions I made was that my scenes had a comparable visual impact to what was already in the piece. It meant going to locations like Blenheim Palace for the big organ, and Syon House in Greenwich and Stowe Castle for this magnificent ballroom sequence, because I wanted my scenes to have all that sort of grandeur.'

True, *The Avengers* does offer the opportunity of seeing Sean Connery dressed as a six-foot-two teddy bear, and it was a welcome change to see this perennial hero tackling the other side of the coin, but on almost every other level *The Avengers* – with a woefully weedy Ralph Fiennes as John Steed and a dreadfully miscast Uma Thurman as Emma Peel – was an unmitigated disaster. Producer Weintraub famously refused to screen the movie for any members of the press worldwide prior to its release, an unprecedented action, with Weintraub claiming it wasn't because the film was bad, it was just that he wanted the audience to 'discover' the film for themselves, without any preconceptions. He was, basically, lying. The movie was terrible and a resounding flop at the box office.

But by this late stage in the game, Sean Connery's stardom was seemingly so unassailable that even one of the biggest flops in recent Hollywood memory (never a very long time, admittedly) did him no harm. If the movie failed, it was someone else's fault, he remained untarnished. He had reached a position that few actors or movie stars before him had reached. And he had never played by the rules to get there.

7. The Politically Incorrect Sexiest Man Alive

Sean Connery saw out the millennium by being named Sexiest Man of the Century. Not bad going for a sixty-nine-year-old former milkman from Fountainbridge. He also departed the twentieth century with two movies that showed – in their own way – just how wilful he could be and generally was. The first saw him forsake his usual billing and fee and take part in a small ensemble drama, playing a man in his sixties, married to his wife for over four decades; the second saw him playing the same age and proving utterly irresistible to a woman nearly forty years his junior.

'I took that role because I fancied something different,' said Connery of *Playing By Heart*, a film for which he dropped his regular $14 million salary down to a rather modest $60,000. 'It's unusual to see a movie about two old-age pensioners who've had a forty-year relationship.' Indeed it is, and it was even more unusual to see Sean Connery playing such a role. While he had never denied his age, he had often used it to point up how vital he still was; here, once again, Connery was

One more before the Millennium – Connery in the 1999 hit Entrapment ☆

Honoured by the Kennedy Centre for the Performing Arts, Washington, December 1999. President Bill Clinton looks on ☆

subtly shifting the audience's perception of him – although not that many turned up to witness it.

One of his co-stars in the movie, Madeleine Stowe, had previously auditioned for the female lead in *Medicine Man*, the role that eventually went to Lorraine Bracco. She had lost that part, after failing to dance well at the audition. This time Connery saw that wasn't an issue. 'He taught me to dance for this film,' Stowe said. 'There's nothing that man can't do.'

And that included convincingly seducing thirty-year-old Catherine Zeta Jones in his next movie, *Entrapment*. A stylish, old-fashioned caper, with both lead actor and actress cast as world-class art thieves, Connery had a strong hand in developing *Entrapment*, which, for the first time, bore the name of his new production company, Fountainbridge Films, a strong sign, if one were needed, that he had no plans to slow things down as his seventieth year on the planet approached.

As ever, he worked extensively on the script and pre-production of the movie, parting ways with the film's first director Antoine Faqua – he wanted all-out action, Connery wanted to emphasize the romance – and hiring Jon Amiel as a replacement The movie opened in the spring of 1999 and was an immediate hit, grabbing the top spot at the US box office and raking in over $21 million in its first weekend, effectively kick-starting the American summer movie season early that year.

In some quarters, however, there were comments made about the significant age gap between the leading man and his leading lady. Australian actor Mel Gibson even spoke out, in a veiled reference to Connery, stating how this growing trend among older actors of casting themselves as romantic leads opposite women young enough to be their granddaughters, was ridiculous and he had no intention of following it himself as age crept up on him.

But Connery didn't concern himself with political correctness. He never had before, so why start now? After all, this was a man who never played by the rules. If he had, he surely would have stayed with Bond. And he certainly wouldn't have spent a significant amount of his time over the years suing most of Hollywood. 'I think Paramount is the only film company I haven't sued,' he said in the late 1980s. 'They all steal.'

Perhaps because of his being a Scot, Connery's dealings with all things financial have always been viewed with intense scrutiny, the actor being described in some quarters (the press) as either 'canny', or 'tight'. Part of this reputation stems from the number of very public finance-based lawsuits he has been involved in, the impact of some of which is still felt in Hollywood today.

Connery, as ever, started at the top. In 1966, while filming *A Fine Madness*, he took legal action against Jack Warner, one of the Warner Bros and therefore one of the most powerful men in the film industry. The movie ran over and the actor demanded $50,000 overtime pay. It could well have been a 'You'll never work in this town again' disaster, but Warner settled.

He followed this in 1969 by suing a French newspaper, *France Soir*, when they claimed he was now too out of shape to play Bond. Using his tailor as a witness to prove that his waistline had expanded by just one inch since he first played 007, the actor, again, won the case.

Two years after filming *The Man Who Would Be King*, Connery (who was about to part from his financial adviser Kenneth Richards and also file action against him) and co-star Michael Caine did some sums and realized they were not being paid their full profit share from John Huston's movie, to the tune of $109,146 each. The two actors promptly took legal action against the film's distributor, Allied Artists.

It was a brave move at a time when studios and distributors were still the dominant force in Hollywood, years before the day of the super-agent and the $20 million-a-movie movie star. The two actors stood to lose more than they could gain, but for both of them it was a matter of principle. The actor was always the one who lost out in such cases, and Connery and Caine were determined to draw a line in the sand. 'Somebody's got to stop them,' Connery reasoned at the time, 'or we're just performing monkeys.'

When the actor made his feelings clear to the press – 'I never cheated anyone in my life. And I don't see why people like myself who really work hard, should be stolen from, cheated and defrauded' – Allied Artists shot back a countersuit claiming $21 million for libel, with a further $10 million demanded in punitive damages from each actor.

Losing the case would've ruined both Caine and Connery, but both men stood their ground. The case went to court in New York where the judge ruled in favour of the actors.

'As usual I had found them stealing,' Connery said, looking back on his victory, 'and it cost me $90,000 to sue them only to prove what was already true. I bankrupted them, I'm thrilled to say.'

It was, in its day, the single most audacious action any actor had taken against the corporate powers that run Hollywood. And it was, naturally, precedent-setting, with numerous stars following the example of the two Brits, inadvertently leading to a revolution in the industry's internal accounting and monitoring systems.

For his next big legal action, Connery again sent shock waves through the film industry. On 20 June 1984, he filed a claim against Cubby Broccoli and United Artists for $225 million, which he deemed to be his share of the fortune that James Bond had made for the producer and the company. His suit also accused Broccoli and UA of breach of contract and of inflicting emotional distress on him. As well reasoned and legally sound as Connery's arguments were, it was clear that there was still a great deal of animosity between him and his old producers, that those feelings he had felt of being exploited – the same thing that had led him to sue Allied Artists – had obviously never left him. It was a move that really could have put his career in jeopardy.

After such a public attack, Connery's case rapidly went underground, where it remained, foraged through by countless legal heads, for several years. Eventually it was settled out of court, with both parties legally bound not to disclose the financial outcome -'And I don't want to breach that, because I've had a career of dealing with lawyers.'

'In films, they keep moving the goalposts every time they make a deal or contract,' Connery said in 1992, offering his view of the Hollywood accounting process. 'It used to be worth something to have a piece of the profits, then it reached the stage where you had to have a piece of the gross, so with that and a lot of other ducking and diving,

Back in traditional garb with wife Micheline ☆

they never let it get into profit and, well, they just steal the money. I've been saying this for so long that it's boring, everybody says he sounds more like an accountant than an actor, but it's so basically and fundamentally wrong. I don't like it, and if someone doesn't keep saying it, it will just get lost under the carpet.'

'Nobody can screw Sean Connery,' offers Terence Young, concisely. 'I think it's almost a religion. He's been screwed and now he can afford the best accountants and the best lawyers to make sure he isn't ever screwed again.'

Connery has also never played it safe politically, and at one time, that also looked to be to his detriment, or at least disappointment. Nominated for a knighthood in 1998 under the Labour government, Connery was passed over for the honour, largely it was felt because of his long-standing support of the Scottish National Party and their plans for an independent Scotland.

'It makes you wonder what exactly is needed to qualify,' he said after hearing the news. 'I wasn't surprised that I didn't get it, so I'm not angry. But I am disappointed in the government's behaviour – I think it lacks class on their part. But it's all because I've been involved with the Scottish National Party for over forty years, and I'm not about to change now. For me, it's simple: if it's called the United

Hail the Conquering Hero ☆

Kingdom, then it should be united. I don't think that between England, Ireland, Wales and Scotland there should be anything less than an equal partnership – which there is not.'

Connery had indeed been involved with the SNP for many years; at one point they had even tried to persuade him to stand as a candidate. Over the intervening decades, Connery's loyalty to his home country had been evidenced by the Scottish

International Education Trust and the vast amounts of money he had raised for this, his most personal of charities. Still, there were those who criticized the man for remaining in exile for purely financial reasons. In the late 1990s, Connery seemed to be addressing that issue – he put his Marbella home on the market and started to look for a property in Scotland. After years in exile, he was coming home. And he was bringing a little piece of Hollywood with him, as Connery became the figurehead of a grand scheme to build a new major film-studio complex in Scotland, funded by Sony and Scottish Screen. 'The reason I want to open a film studio in Scotland is simple: there isn't one. And there's no British film industry to speak of either. It would be a great starting point to have a triangle of Pinewood, Shepperton and an international state-of-the-art studio in Edinburgh. Hopefully, it would act as a massive boost to the industry and I very much want to be involved in that.'

As Sean Connery approached his seventieth year, it became apparent that he was still the man he had always been. The offer was now as it had been back on that day when he marched out of Cubby Broccoli and Harry Saltzman's office: what you see is what you get, and if you want what you see, then you come to Connery. On his terms.

And so it was, that in the 1999 New Year's Honours List, the Labour Party tacitly acknowledged their faux pas of the year before and awarded the SNP supporting actor the opportunity to bear the legend 'Sir' before his name. As the twenty-first century dawned the man who had played kings, who had played men who would be kings, immortals, Greek warriors, cat burglars and superspies, became a Knight.

'If I were to think of how far I've come. How much fame one's had, how much money one's made, one would think – well, it wouldn't be physically possible, considering where I've come from,' he summed up. 'I didn't have anything resembling a great game plan. Everybody claimed that they knew that the James Bond films were going to be a successful series – it's just not true. If you had asked me when I was twenty eight, I definitely wouldn't have imagined I'd still be acting.

'As for looking to the future, I always wanted to be an old man with a good face, like Hitchcock or Picasso. I'm incredibly lucky to still be around, doing all the things I want to do and getting extremely well paid for it. There's a parallel with golf – a lot of it is in the mind, and the moment you start to lose the enthusiasm or appetite, it affects your judgements and decisions. And then you stop performing well. I think enthusiasm and appetite are more important than anything.'

Filmography

Lilacs in the Spring (1954 – unbilled)
Director: Charles Walters
Cast: Leslie Caron, Mel Ferrer, Zsa Zsa Gabor,
Jean-Pierre Aumont, Amanda Blake, Kurt Kaznar

No Road Back (1956)
Director: Montgomery Tully
Cast: Skip Homier, Paul Carpenter, Patricia
Dainton, Norman Wooland, Margaret Rawlins

Hell Drivers (1956)
Director: Cy Endfield
Cast: Stanley Baker, Herbert Lom, Patrick
Mc Goohan, Jill Ireland, Gordon Jackson

Time Lock (1957)
Director: Gerald Thomas
Cast: Robert Beatty, Betty McDowell, Vincent
Winter, Lee Patterson, Peter Mannering

Action of the Tiger (1957)
Director: Terence Young
Cast: Van Johnson, Martine Carol, Herbert Lom,
Anna Gerber

Another Time, Another Place (1958)
Director: Lewis Allen
Cast: Lana Turner, Barry Sullivan, Glynis Johns

Darby O'Gill and the Little People (1959)
Director: Robert Stevenson
Cast: Albert Sharpe, Janet Munro, Jimmy O'Dea,
Kieron Moore, Estelle Winwood

Tarzan's Greatest Adventure (1959)
Director: John Guillermin
Cast: Gordon Scott, Anthony Quayle, Sara Shane,
Niall MacGinnis, Scilla Gabel

The Frightened City (1961)
Director: John Lemont
Cast: Herbert Lom, John Gregson, Alfred Marks,
Yvonne Romain

On the Fiddle (1961) (aka *Operation Snafu* and
Operation Warhead)
Director: Cyril Frankl
Cast: Alfred Lynch, Cecil Parker, Stanley
Holloway, Alan King, Wilfrid Hyde White

The Longest Day (1962)
Director: Ken Annakin
Cast: Andrew Marton, Bernhard Wicki, John
Wayne, Rod Steiger, Robert Ryan, Peter Lawford,
Henry Fonda

Dr No (1962)
Director: Terence Young
Cast: Ursula Andress, Joseph Whiteman, Jack
Lord, Bernard Lee, Lois Maxwell

Four beers down ☆

From Russia With Love (1963)
Director: Terence Young
Cast: Daniela Bianchi, Lotte Lenya, Pedro
Armendariz, Robert Shaw, Bernard Lee, Lois
Maxwell

Woman of Straw (1964)
Director: Basil Dearden
Cast: Gina Lollobrigida, Ralph Richardson, John
Sekka, Alexander Knox

Marnie (1964)
Director: Alfred Hitchcock
Cast: Tippi Hedren, Diane Baker, Martin Gabel,
Louise Latham, Alan Napier

Goldfinger (1964)
Director: Guy Hamilton
Cast: Gert Frobe, Honor Blackman, Shirley Eaton,
Bernard Lee, Lois Maxwell, Harold Sakata

The Hill (1965)
Director: Sidney Lumet
Cast: Harry Andrews, Ian Hendry, Michael
Redgrave, Ian Bannen, Ossie Davis, Alfred Lynch

Thunderball (1965)
Director: Terence Young
Cast: Claudine Auger, Adolfo Celi, Luciana
Paluzzi, Rik Van Nutter, Martine Beswick

007 & DB5 ☆

A Fine Madness (1966)
Director: Irvin Kershner
Cast: Joanne Woodward, Jean Seberg, Patrick
O'Neill, Coleen Dewhurst, Renee Taylor

You Only Live Twice (1967)
Director: Lewis Gilbert
Cast: Akiko Wakabayashi, Donald Pleasence,
Tetsuro Tamba, Mie Hama, Teru Shimada, Karin
Dor, Lois Maxwell

The Bowler and the Bunnet (1967; TV; director
only)

Shalako (1968)
Director: Edward Dimytryk
Cast: Brigitte Bardot, Stephen Boyd, Jack
Hawkins, Peter Van Eyck, Honor Blackman

The Molly Maguires (1969)
Director: Martin Ritt
Cast: Richard Harris, Samantha Eggar, Frank
Finlay, Art Lund, Anthony Costello

The Red Tent (1970)
Director: Mickail K. Kalatozov
Cast: Claudia Cardinale, Hardy Kruger, Peter Finch,
Massimo Girotti, Luigi Vannucchi, Mario Adorf

The Anderson Tapes (1971)
Director: Sidney Lumet
Cast: Dyan Cannon, Martin Balsam, Ralph Meeker,
Alan King, Margaret Hamilton, Christopher Walken,
Garret Morris

Diamonds Are Forever (1971)
Director: Guy Hamilton
Cast: Jill St John, Charles Gray, Lana Wood, Jimmy
Dean, Bruce Cabot, Putter Smith

The Offence (1972)
Director: Sidney Lumet
Cast: Trevor Howard, Vivien Merchant, Ian
Bannen, Derek Newark

Zardoz (1973)
Director: John Boorman
Cast: Charlotte Rampling, Sara Kestelman, Sally
Anne Newton, John Alderton, Niall Buggy

Ransom (1974) (aka *The Terrorists*)
Director: Caspar Wrede
Cast Norman Bristow, Richard Harris, Ian
McShane, John Cording, Isabel Dean

Murder on the Orient Express (1974)
Director: Sidney Lumet
Cast: Albert Finney, Lauren Bacall, Martin Balsam,
Ingrid Bergman, Jacqueline Bisset

The Wind and the Lion (1975)
Director: John Milius
Cast: Candice Bergen, Brian Keith, John Huston,
Geoffrey Lewis, Steve Kanaly, Vladek Sheybal

The Man Who Would Be King (1975)
Director: John Huston
Cast: Michael Caine, Christopher Plummer, Saeed
Jaffrey, Shakira Caine

Robin and Marian (1976)
Director: Richard Lester
Cast: Audrey Hepburn, Robert Shaw, Richard
Harris, Nicol Williamson, Denholm Elliott

The Next Man (1976)
Director: Richard C. Sarafin
Cast: Cornelia Sharpe, Albert Paulsen, Adolfo Celi

A Bridge Too Far (1977)
Director: Richard Attenborough
Cast: Dirk Bogarde, James Caan, Michael Caine,
Edward Fox, Elliott Gould

The First Great Train Robbery (1978)
Director: Michael Crichton
Cast: Donald Sutherland, Lesley Anne-Down, Alan
Webb, Malcom Terris, Wayne Sleep, Robert Lang

Meteor (1979)
Director: Ronald Neame
Cast: Natalie Wood, Karl Malden, Brian Keith,
Henry Fonda, Martin Landau, Trevor Howard

Cuba (1979)
Director: Richard Lester
Cast: Brooke Adams, Jack Weston, Hector Elizondo,
Denholm Elliott, Chris Sarandon, Lonette McKee

Time Bandits (1981)
Director: Terry Gilliam
Cast: Shelly Duvall, John Cleese, Kathryn Helmond,
Ian Holm, Michael Palin, Ralph Richardson, Peter
Vaughn, David Rappaport

Outland (1981)
Director: Peter Hyams
Cast: Peter Boyle, Frances Sternhagen, James B.
Sikking, Kika Markham, Clarke Peters, John
Ratzenberger

Wrong Is Right (aka *The Man with the Deadly
Lens*) (1982)
Director: Richard Brooks
Cast: George Grizzard, Robert Conrad, Katherine
Ross, G. D. Spradlin, John Saxon, Henry Silva,
Leslie Nielsen, Robert Webber

Five Days One Summer (1982)
Director: Fred Zinneman
Cast: Betsy Brantley, Lambert Wilson, Jennifer
Hilary, Isabel Dean, Gerald Burh, Anna Massey

The Sword of the Valiant (1982)
Director: Stephen Weeks
Cast: Miles O'Keeffe, Cyrielle Claire, Leigh Lawson,
Trevor Howard, Peter Cushing, Ronald Lacey, Lila
Kedrova

Never Say Never Again (1983)
Director: Irvin Kershner
Cast: Klaus Maria Brandauer, Max Von Sydow,
Barbara Carrera, Kim Basinger, Bernie Casey, Alec
McCowen, Edward Fox

Highlander (1986)
Director: Russell Mulcahy
Cast: Christopher Lambert, Roxanne Hart, Clancy
Brown, Beatie Edney, Alan North

The Name of the Rose (1986)
Director: Jean Jacques Annaud
Cast: F. Murray Abraham, Christian Slater, Elya
Baskin, Feodor Chaliapin Jr, William Hickey,
Michael Lonsdale, Ron Perlman

The Untouchables (1987)
Director: Brian De Palma
Cast: Kevin Costner, Charles Martin Smith, Andy
Garcia, Robert De Niro, Richard Bradford, Jack
Kehoe, Brad Sullivan, Billy Drago, Patricia Clarkson

The Presidio (1988)
Director: Peter Hyams
Cast: Mark Harmon, Meg Ryan, Jack Warden, Mark
Blum, Dana Gladstone, Jenette Goldstein, Don Calfa

Memories of Me (1988 – as himself)
Director: Henry Winkler
Cast: Billy Crystal, Alan King, Michael Hertzberg

Indiana Jones and the Last Crusade (1989)
Director: Steven Spielberg
Cast: Harrison Ford, Kate Capshaw, Ke Huy Quan,
Amrish Puri, Roshan Seth, Philip Stone, Dan
Ackroyd

Family Business (1989)
Director: Sidney Lumet
Cast: Dustin Hoffman, Matthew Broderick, Rosana
de Soto, Janet Carroll, Victoria Jackson, Bill
McCutcheon, Deborah Rush, Brainy Broderick

The Hunt for Red October (1990)
Director: John McTiernan
Cast: Alec Baldwin, Scott Glenn, Sam Neill, James
Earl Jones, Joss Ackland, Richard Jordan, Peter Firth,
Tim Curry

The Russia House (1990)
Director: Fred Schepisi
Cast: Michelle Pfeiffer, Roy Scheider, James Fox,
Klaus Maria Brandauer, John Mahoney, Michael
Kitchen

Highlander II – The Quickening (1990)
Director: Russell Mulcahy
Cast: Christopher Lambert, Virginia Madsen, Michael
Ironside, John C. McGinley, Allan Rich, Phil Brock

Robin Hood: Prince of Thieves (1991)
Director: Kevin Reynolds
Cast: Kevin Costner, Morgan Freeman, Mary
Elizabeth Mastrantonio, Christian Slater, Alan
Rickman, Geraldine McEwan

*Sharp in a suit – not
always great with hats* ☆

Medicine Man (1992)
Director: John McTiernan
Cast: Lorraine Bracco. Jose Wilker

Rising Sun (1993)
Director: Philip Kaufman
Cast: Wesley Snipes, Harvey Keitel. Cary-Hiroyuki
Tagawa, Kevin Anderson Mako. Ray Wise, Stan
Egi, Stan Shaw, Tia Carrere

A Good Man in Africa (1994)
Director: Bruce Beresford
Cast: Colin Friels, Joanne Whalley-Kilmer. John
Lithgow. Louis Gossett Jr. Diana Rigg. Sarah-Jane
Fenton

Just Cause (1995)
Director: Arne Glimcher
Cast: Laurence Fishburne, Kate Capshaw. Blair
Underwood, Ed Harris. Christopher Murray, Ruby
Dee

First Knight (1995)
Director: Jerry Zucker
Cast: Richard Gere, Julia Ormond, Ben Cross

The Rock (1996)
Director: Michael Bay
Cast: Nicholas Cage. Ed Harris. Michael Biehn.
William Forsythe. David Morse. John Spencer

Dragonheart (voice only: 1996)
Director: Rob Cohen
Cast: Dennis Quaid, David Thewlis. Dina Meyer.
Julie Christie. Pete Postlethwaite. Jason Isaacs

The Avengers (1998)
Director: Jeremiah Chechick
Cast: Ralph Fiennes. Uma Thurman. Fiona Shaw.
Jim Broadbent. Eddie Izzard. Eileen Atkins

Playing by Heart (1999)
Director: Willard Carroll
Cast: Gillian Anderson. Ellen Burstyn. Anthony
Edwards. Angelina Jolie. Dennis Quaid. Gena
Rowlands. Madeline Stowe

Entrapment (1999)
Director: Jon Amiel
Cast: Catherine Zeta Jones, Ving Rhames, Will
Patton. Maury Chaykin. Terry O'Neill

Index

Page numbers in *italic* refer to illustrations

Bibliography

Richard Gant, *Sean Connery: Gilt Edge Bond*, Mayflower, 1967

Robert Sellers, *Sean Connery: A Celebration*, 1999

John Parker, *Sean Connery*, Victor Gollancz, 1993

Kenneth Passingham, *Sean Connery*, Sidgwick & Jackson, 1983

Michael Caine, *What's It All About?*, Arrow, 1992

Robert Sellers, *Harrison Ford*, Warner Books, 1987

Sources

Empire, Premiere, Sight & Sound, Films & Filming, Cinefantastique, Photoplay, TV Times, Radio Times, Prevue, Films Illustrated, Screen International, Variety, Starburst, Time Out, Hollywood Reporter, American Film, Interview, Broadcast, Film Comment, Vanity Fair, Film Review, Monthly Film Bulletin

Sunday Times, Sunday Express, Daily Express, Daily Mirror, Daily Telegraph, Guardian, Evening News, Evening Standard

Illustrations

Every reasonable effort has been made to acknowledge the ownership of copyrighted photographs included in this volume. Any errors that have inadvertently occurred will be corrected in subsequent editions provided notification is sent to the publisher.

Alpha: pages 87 (right), 88, 94, 95, 114, 120, 131, 149 **Corbis/Everett Collection:** 6, 9, 23, 39, 52–3, 55, 81 (bottom left), 83 (bottom right), 97, 123, 136, 150, 152, 154, 157, 158, 161 **Eon/Kobal:** 37, 60–61, 71, 83 (top right), 84 (top), 98, 127, 132, 142 **Hulton Getty:** 24, 58, 65, 82, 90, 92, 109 **Mander & Mitchenson:** 17, 47 **Mirror Syndication:** 15 **Pictorial Press:** 2, 20, 34, 43, 48, 51, 56, 62, 63, 66, 67, 68, 72, 75, 76, 79, 80, 81 (top left), 81 (right), 83 (left), 84 (bottom left), 85, 86 (top), 86 (bottom), 91, 100, 103, 104, 110, 113, 117, 118, 124, 128, 133, 134, 139, 141, 145, 146 **Ronald Grant Archive:** 19, 27, 28, 30, 32, 33, 40, 87 (left), 107 **Vin Mag:** 10, 13

Acknowledgements

The author would like to thank the following: Sean Connery (for Christmas and New Year!), the team at Essential Books (for the same, and more), Rob Churchill (for spare change and company), Ian Watson (for his Goldfinger), Kelly Osborn (for her video card), Mary McCabe (for being a mum), Paul Gillion (for being a friend), Michael Samuels (for being himself – and I think, also for fifty quid early on), Terry Gilliam (for tea and reminiscences), Prince (for the early years before he went weird) and the BFI Library, as always, for their untiring help (especially the tall bald guy).

BM, somewhat unexpectedly in the twenty-first century